ℰ

· · · · · · · · · · · · · · · ·

ARE
YOU A
Jackie
OR A
Marilyn?

· · · · · · · · · · · · · · · ·

ℰ

GOTHAM BOOKS

ARE YOU A

JACKIE

OR A

MARILYN?

TIMELESS LESSONS
ON LOVE, POWER,
AND STYLE

PAMELA KEOGH

GOTHAM BOOKS
Published by Penguin Group (USA) Inc.
375 Hudson Street, New York, New York 10014, U.S.A.
Penguin Group (Canada), 90 Eglinton Avenue East, Suite 700, Toronto, Ontario M4P 2Y3, Canada (a division of Pearson Penguin Canada Inc.); Penguin Books Ltd, 80 Strand, London WC2R 0RL, England; Penguin Ireland, 25 St Stephen's Green, Dublin 2, Ireland (a division of Penguin Books Ltd); Penguin Group (Australia), 250 Camberwell Road, Camberwell, Victoria 3124, Australia (a division of Pearson Australia Group Pty Ltd); Penguin Books India Pvt Ltd, 11 Community Centre, Panchsheel Park, New Delhi—110 017, India; Penguin Group (NZ), 67 Apollo Drive, Rosedale, North Shore 0632, New Zealand (a division of Pearson New Zealand Ltd); Penguin Books (South Africa) (Pty) Ltd, 24 Sturdee Avenue, Rosebank, Johannesburg 2196, South Africa

Penguin Books Ltd, Registered Offices: 80 Strand, London WC2R 0RL, England

Published by Gotham Books, a member of Penguin Group (USA) Inc.

First printing, October 2010
10 9 8 7 6 5 4 3 2 1

Gotham Books and the skyscraper logo are trademarks of Penguin Group (USA) Inc.

LIBRARY OF CONGRESS CATALOGING-IN-PUBLICATION DATA
Keogh, Pamela Clarke.
    Are you a Jackie or a Marilyn? : timeless lessons on love, power and style / Pamela Keogh.
        p. cm.
    ISBN 978-1-59240-569-5 (hardcover)
    1. Beauty, Personal. 2. Feminine beauty (Aesthetics) 3. Monroe, Marilyn, 1926–1962.
4. Onassis, Jacqueline Kennedy, 1929–1994. I. Title.
    HQ1219.K46 2010
    646.7'042—dc22   2010015286

ISBN 978-1-592-40569-5

Printed in the United States of America
Set in Sabon
Designed by Spring Hoteling
Illustrations by Meg Hess

*For Lauren Marino, who saw this book before I did,
and
Terri Austin Keogh—
a great friend who is both Jackie and Marilyn.*

Contents

*I*ntroduction

"*A*re you a Jackie or a Marilyn?"

Jacqueline Kennedy Onassis and Marilyn Monroe are two of the most memorable women to have graced our cultural—and visual—landscape in modern times. Both were legendary, but in completely different ways, and they represent opposite possibilities for modern women to aspire to, even today.

Jackie or Marilyn—at first glance, it seems so simple, doesn't it?

The first lady versus the Hollywood starlet. The Vassar girl versus the teenager who dropped out of Hollywood High after six months. The woman from a "good family" (and all that entails) from Washington, D.C.; Newport, Rhode Island; Southampton, New York—with occasional forays to Europe—versus the woman from the Los Angeles Orphans Home and a hundred film sets, scrapping her way up the ladder.

Are they alike? Are they different? And more important, how do they speak to us today?

*J*acqueline Bouvier Kennedy Onassis was born on July 28, 1929, in Southampton, New York, where her parents spent the summer. While the Kennedys might be described as "American royalty" by well-meaning journalists, Jackie and the Bouvier clan were (on technical points) several rungs up the social ladder and far more royal than her future in-laws. Born into the *Social Register* and (although Catholic) part of the elite, regimented and very restricted WASP aristocracy, Jackie was first introduced to the American public in 1953, after marrying Senator John F. Kennedy, and became widely known while campaigning for her husband's bid for presidency.

When he won the election in 1960 (by the slimmest margin in the 20th century), Jackie—stylish, chic and very much the anti–Mamie Eisenhower (her predecessor)—burst onto the world stage as the wife of the thirty-fifth president of the United States, and the media breathlessly followed her every move.

When Jackie wore a sleeveless sheath dress and bare legs (a teenage girl or woman not wearing stockings in public just wasn't done in those days) to Sunday Mass in Palm Beach, it caused an uproar, and millions of women quickly followed suit. Her bouffant hairdo and her habit of wearing jodhpurs as sportswear and a triple-strand pearl necklace tucked into the neckline of her dress were all instantly copied.

Among the first celebrities not based on the stage or screen, Jackie and her husband lifted the curtain on the American upper class and disseminated East Coast style throughout the country and the world.

After John F. Kennedy was assassinated on November 22, 1963, Jackie rebuilt a life for herself and her children, Caroline and John Junior, in New York City. In 1968, she married the Greek shipping magnate Aristotle Onassis, earning the ire of the world. After his death in 1975, she settled permanently in Manhattan and began working as a book editor at Doubleday publishers. As the most famous woman in the world, Jackie made news with every move.

*G*rowing up and throughout her life, Jackie had every imaginable advantage—gracious homes with staff and her own horse, the best education possible, a father who doted on her and husbands who protected her. But perhaps the most important thing Jackie had was a center, a clear identity: She knew who she was and her place in the world.

Marilyn, on the other hand, had none of these advantages. For starters, not even the name "Marilyn Monroe" was originally her own. Instead, it was a studio invention.

Three years older than Jackie, Marilyn was born Norma Jeane Mortenson on June 1, 1926, in Los Angeles, California, to Gladys Baker, an unmarried woman with deep psychological problems who worked as a film cutter at RKO studios. The identity of Marilyn's father was never made known to her (in later life, she claimed to remember a photograph of a handsome man with a mustache), and she was later baptized Norma Jeane Baker.

Unlike Jackie's, Norma Jeane's childhood was uncertain and, at times, harrowing. She had a clear memory of her mother having a fit and being taken out of the house in a straitjacket, and for the rest of her life, she feared that she might end up the same way.

On June 19, 1942, she wed her twenty-one-year-old neighbor, Jimmy Dougherty, whom she barely knew. It is said that Norma Jeane was weeping when her husband left, having been drafted during World War II. A few months later she was discovered while working in a wartime factory and found an even greater love: the camera.

Marilyn's will was formidable; her desire, immense. She wanted, she wanted, she wanted.

She wanted respect. She wanted love. She would marry and divorce twice more. She wanted a home and a loving husband, children even. She wanted to be a world-famous movie star; she fought for decent scripts. In retrospect, when she was recognized all over the world—our blonde bombshell goddess, Marilyn—it all seemed inevitable.

Perhaps it was.

And yet. . . . While Jackie had every societal advantage and Marilyn so many strikes against her in her birth, they were more than equal in the fame game. Although Jackie lived a longer life, Marilyn is perhaps more beloved today because people all over the world connect with her on an emotional level. Her desire to be known, to be loved, is as much a part of her appeal as her innocent sexuality.

Jackie and Marilyn came of age in the 1950s, when socially acceptable roles for women were limited: wife and mother (the best), and if you had to work, schoolteacher or nurse. Or maybe waitress or secretary. That's about it.

Yet they both moved beyond the strictures of their time and became icons—the free-spirited movie star and the cosmopolitan first lady. If Jackie symbolized well-bred propriety, Marilyn *was* sex.

Jackie and Marilyn, it seems, ascribed to their public personas. It is no wonder that in the second season of *Mad Men,* where all of the women in Don Draper's world are either Madonnas or whores, the ad campaign they came up with for Playtex included photos of two models side by side in their brassieres. One was a "Jackie." The other was a "Marilyn"— and you can guess which was which.

While this limited way of thinking dictates that women are one or the other, the fact is that most of us, really, are a mixture of both.

The question "Are you a Jackie or a Marilyn?" seems simple enough, but like the two women it is based on—Jacqueline Kennedy Onassis and Marilyn Monroe—the answer is often far more complex and not so obvious as might first appear.

The Jackie Woman we envision is strong, intelligent, socially impeccable, well married, probably a mother and can take care of herself and others. The Marilyn Gal is vulnerable, emotionally unbalanced, enjoys sex immensely, with lots of beauty, sorrow, pills, high living, celebrity, glamour, black eyeliner, fake eyelashes and champagne in her day-to-day existence. Plus, you know she's got some beautiful, beautiful photographs of herself stashed away.

In today's celebrity world, the comparison might be Jennifer Garner versus Kate Moss, or Reese Witherspoon compared to, say, Amy Winehouse.

Among women we love, let's take Tina Turner as an example. With her perfect legs, fringed miniskirts (that she has been rocking since about 1967) and daunting sexual energy, she might appear to be a Marilyn. But looking beyond first impressions to her courage, strength and personal work ethic, she is actually a Jackie.

Her heir apparent of today, Beyoncé Knowles, is the rare pop icon who combines discipline, talent and a wholesome sexual energy to present herself as a combination of both Jackie and Marilyn.

On the other side of the spectrum, classic style icon Grace Kelly was extremely Marilyn-esque before her marriage, but as she settled into an almost suburban existence as Her Royal Highness Princess Grace of Monaco, she became more and more personally conservative until she was even less a Jackie than the real Jackie herself.

*B*ut like so many things in life, the answer to whether one is a Jackie or a Marilyn is not black and white. Human beings are complex creatures (especially *you*), and there is a broad spectrum within which one can fall; we are not necessarily one or the other—the Jackie/Marilyn hybrid, if you will. And at the risk of becoming too schizophrenic, this option could very well be the best of both worlds, because clearly, the choice between being a Jackie or a Marilyn depends on the situation.

(And here's something else we've noticed: Whether you are a Jackie or a Marilyn, you are always a bit of an actress. You might be studying at the Actors Studio, or you might work at the Genius Bar of the Apple store or as a teller in a bank. You could be a stay-at-home mom or married to the president of the United States. In your mind, it's all shades of the same inherently fabulous "look at me!" energy—just the venue is different.)

For the J+M Gal of today, it's all about style, attitude and behavior . . . and then channeling (if only in your mind) your favorite icon. You might even mix it up a little. If you are going on a job interview: Jackie. Going to Vegas: Marilyn. Going on a job interview *in* Vegas? More Marilyn with a touch of Jackie.

Meeting your future mother-in-law for the first time? Definitely Jackie.

Going to Paris for a long weekend with the new beau? Jackie with a soupçon of Marilyn (and if you are staying at the Georges V, feel free to pour on the Marilyn with abandon).

*T*he mind boggles. Which is why you need this handy primer to make your way in the world. After studying the underlying habits, belief systems, fashion advice and sexual energy (oh, you knew we'd get there eventually) of both JKO and MM, we will determine whether you are a Jackie or a Marilyn (or somewhere in between). So consider this your go-to guide for being a retro-modern woman. It's all here, from finding your style to feathering your nest. From courtship to sex and beauty, we have advice on how to write a love letter, how to stock a bar, how to ask for a raise, even what books, CDs and DVDs the Jackie or Marilyn Gal—i.e., *you*—might favor. We cover all the bases, from soup to nuts. We're in your boudoir, we're in your office and we're on your first date—and the third. We have recipes, historical references, real-life situations, diet tips and even some great gossip.

Finally, we know that the Jackie/Marilyn Woman has courage and style in spades. Even better, we can show you how to recognize it in yourself and bring out your inner Jackie or Marilyn in any situation.

*S*o—*are* you a Jackie or a Marilyn? By the time you finish reading this book, you might find that there is less than you might imagine separating the two. And whether you favor ballet flats, kitten heels, marabou mules, Converse sneakers or sky-high stilettos, we will show you how to throw the dice, take chances and sashay down the sidewalk of life with more style than you can imagine.

*J*ust like our girls Jackie and Marilyn. And now you.

THE JACKIE OR MARILYN QUIZ

In pondering the essential differences between the Jackie and the Marilyn Gal (with their attendant lifestyles, first husbands, lingerie and heel choices), it is first vital to ascertain whether you are a Jackie or a Marilyn.

Herewith a test.

And in case you are wondering, the Jackie among us is a test taker nonpareil, who would fill this out very fast, with perfect concentration and a perfectly sharpened No. 2 Ticonderoga pencil. And the Marilyn? Distractedly (no doubt wearing a sheer peignoir), with an eyebrow pencil fished out from the bottom of her purse—but she would look *adorable* mulling it over.

1. Who said, "All men are rats and cannot be trusted"?

   a) Jackie's father, John "Black Jack" Bouvier

   b) Gloria Steinem

   c) Marilyn Monroe in *Some Like It Hot*

2. Who said, "Just give me champagne and good food and I'm in heaven and love"?

   a) Oprah Winfrey

   b) Ina Garten

   c) Marilyn Monroe

3. Of these modern-day celebrities, who is the least Marilyn-esque?

   a) Madonna

   b) Scarlett Johansson

   c) Lindsay Lohan

4. During times of stress, do you—

   a) go for a walk on the beach.

   b) meditate.

   c) pour gin in your tea.

5. For you, sex is—

   a) uncomplicated and fun!

   b) a way of saying "thank you."

   c) a means to an end.

6. Before you meet a man for dinner, you—

   a) shave your legs

   b) run a Dun & Bradstreet on the guy.

   c) break out your tippy-tallest Manolos and hope for the best.

7. You wake up every morning—

   a) with your day completely planned.

   b) and do whatever you feel like.

   c) turn to the person next to you and say, "Hello, dear."

8. Your childhood is something—

   a) not discussed.

   b) to be celebrated.

   c) you've been running from your whole life.

9. Your father—

   a) loved you and gave you confidence.

   b) was Clark Gable.

   c) taught you to throw a football.

10. Your mother—

    a) scares the hell out of you.

    b) left you all of her Balenciaga and Schlumberger.

    c) secretly loves your little sister (you know, the "pretty one") more.

11. After you sleep with someone for the first time, he—

    a) offers you the lead in his movie.

    b) asks you to marry him.

    c) has a Cartier bibelot on the breakfast tray.

12. In your opinion, money is—

    a) everything.

    b) no, we mean it—*everything*.

    c) not that important—as long as you have a roof over your head and Veuve Clicquot in the fridge, you're cool.

13. Meeting your future mother-in-law for the first time, you—

    a) convert to Judaism.

    b) brush up on your French.

    c) eschew underwear.

14. Former beaux keep up with you—

    a) on Facebook.

    b) on the front page of the *New York Times*.

    c) They don't. They're still devastated by the breakup. They'll never get over it. Never.

15. You best friend is—

    a) your roommate from prep school.

    b) your hairdresser, makeup artist, stand-in, publicist, housekeeper, majordomo, Peggy Siegal—or some varying combination of the above.

    c) just you, baby. Just you.

16. Questions for general discussion—Is it better to be a Jackie or a Marilyn—

if you are in the running for first lady of the United States?

in bed with a handsome stranger you will never see again?

in bed with a French couturier?

lunching at Bailey's Beach?

on the proverbial (or not so proverbial) casting couch?

applying to Vassar?

on a photo shoot with Bert Stern, a case of champagne and immortality?

Answers—1) a—Black Jack Bouvier; **2)** c—Marilyn Monroe; **3)** a—Madonna—while she may have looked like MM in her youth, her MO is pure JKO; **4)** a—Jackie; b—Jackie; c—Marilyn; **5)** a—Marilyn; b—Marilyn; c—Jackie; **6)** a—Marilyn; b—Jackie; c—Marilyn; **7)** a—Jackie; b—Marilyn; c) either; **8)** a—Marilyn; b—Jackie; c—Marilyn; **9)** a—Jackie; b—Marilyn; c—neither; **10)** a—either; b—Jackie; c—Jackie; **11)** a—Marilyn; b—Marilyn; c—Jackie; **12)** a—Jackie; b—Jackie; c—Marilyn; **13)** a—Marilyn; b—Jackie; c—Marilyn (of course); **14)** a—neither; b—either; c—Marilyn; **15)** a—Jackie; b—Marilyn; c—Marilyn.

To Determine Scoring—Tally up your responses, giving yourself one "Jackie" point for each question you answered about her correctly and one "Marilyn" point for each correct Marilyn answer. Whichever score is highest corresponds to your predominant archetype. In case of a tie, you are either kidding yourself or are Uma Thurman.

"No one ever told me I was pretty when I was a little girl. All little girls should be told they're pretty, even if they aren't."

—MM

. . . .

"I like to use the word original in describing Jacqueline. . . . She was very intense and felt strongly about things. . . ."

—JANET LEE AUCHINCLOSS, JKO'S MOTHER

The number-one rule for living like a Jackie or a Marilyn (or some combination thereof) is to create yourself in your own (best) image.

Infamous paparazzo Ron Galella (who bugged the heck out of stars like Jackie, Robert Redford and Marlon Brando but has some amazing photographs to show for it) described the transformation of Jackie and Marilyn. "They were both actresses—they both created themselves. Jackie created an aura, and she kept people at a distance with her whispery voice. She really wasn't out there as much. She was a mystery. Marilyn was more obvious, straightforward. As far as being sexy—she had it over Jackie. *Way* over Jackie."

And don't let something as minor as a lack of education (MM), social background (MM) or a challenging childhood (JKO/MM) deter you from your particular vision. F. Scott Fitzgerald had it wrong when he said, "There are no second acts." This is America after all, where people straining the outer boundaries of late middle age are capable of saying "sixty is the new forty" with a straight face (and meaning it). We practically invented the third, fourth and fifth act.

In fact, we encourage you to be whatever you want—it can change from day to day, even from hour to hour. The most important thing is, you're in control.

J+M LIFE LESSONS

The Jackie Life Lesson—Remake Your Past
The Marilyn Life Lesson—Run from Your Childhood. Fast.

*W*hile Jackie had the typically strict (and somewhat neglected) upbringing of her upper-class milieu (noted for its emphasis on horseback-riding skills, attracting suitable beaux, attention to clothes and maintaining slimness), Marilyn Monroe's childhood was so bereft it was Dickensian.

Unlike Jackie, Marilyn was raised on the outskirts of society in foster homes and orphanages until 1937, when she moved in with a friend of her mother's, Grace McKee Goddard. Her time with Mrs. Goddard and her husband was happy—Grace loved the movies, and she and Norma Jeane would spend afternoons in the theater watching Jean Harlow. She also encouraged Norma Jeane to wear powder and makeup and took her to the hair salon to get her hair done. Unfortunately, when Grace's husband was transferred to the East Coast in 1942, the couple could not afford to bring the sixteen-year-old Norma Jeane with them, and Norma Jeane was given two options: return to the orphanage (a place she hated) or get married.

With a mentally unstable mother, a history of sexual abuse and a succession of increasingly negligent foster-home situations, Marilyn was born so far behind the eight ball, one cannot help but root for her.

Almost through dint of will, both Jackie and Marilyn remade themselves in the image of they wanted to be—and again, Marilyn's childhood experience was exponentially worse than Jackie's—but the lesson is that whether you are a Jackie or a Marilyn, you can, too.

Let's start at the beginning, and that is—

RECAST YOUR CHILDHOOD

When reordering your childhood under the Jackie/Marilyn model, you have several different options on how to present yourself. You might decide to be like Jackie and stick to your story or, perhaps, be like Marilyn and tell lots of different stories about your childhood (or really, like any good actress, just the one that serves your purpose at the moment). If all else fails, you can always fall back on the perennial celebrity favorite—lie.

Bob Dylan, for example, claimed to be an orphan (always a favorite among the future famous) who ran away and joined the circus. In actuality, he was born Robert Zimmerman and grew up in stable, middle-class surroundings in Hibbing, Minnesota, and yes, both of his parents were very much alive when they read the whole orphan/circus thing.

Jackie's father, John "Black Jack" Bouvier, presented by her as a glamorous roué, was—when seen in another light—a crippling alcoholic with father/daughter boundary issues, as well as a dissolute spendthrift incapable of remaining faithful in a marriage, who got so intoxicated the night before Jackie's wedding, he was unable to walk her down the aisle.

Overlooking all of this, Jackie adored him and placed him on a pedestal—in direct opposition to her strict, spoilsport mother. One of her prized possessions that she kept her entire life was his French Empire desk.[1] When he died in 1957, she had her husband, then Senator Kennedy, hand deliver his obituary (which she wrote) to the *New York Times* so that her father would be properly recognized.

She even planned his funeral. "I want everything to look like a summer garden. Like Lasata in August,"[2] she told her baffled aunts, going so far as to blanket his coffin with bachelor's buttons at the gravesite.

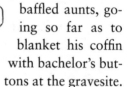

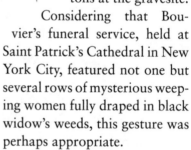

Considering that Bouvier's funeral service, held at Saint Patrick's Cathedral in New York City, featured not one but several rows of mysterious weeping women fully draped in black widow's weeds, this gesture was perhaps appropriate.

During her early years, because of her mother's mental instability and the fact that she grew up without a family, Marilyn was a ward of the state and raised by several foster families. Some were well intentioned, others abusive.[3] (In later years, she would confide in her psychiatrist, Dr. Ralph Greenson, that a boarder at one of her foster homes had sexually abused her beginning at the age of seven, and that when she told her foster mother about it, she did not believe her.) Between stints at

. . . .

1 It was sold at a Sotheby's auction after her death for $70,000.
2 Lasata was the name of the Bouvier estate in the Hamptons. It was purchased in 2007 by Reed Krakoff, president and CEO of Coach, for $24,000,000.
3 As Marilyn was a child of the Depression, it was also intimated that several families took in children purely for financial gain, rather than for any altruistic reasons.

foster homes, she also spent time at the Los Angeles Orphans Home (later renamed Hollygrove), a place she hated. (Some biographies say that she was treated with love and respect there, so it is difficult to figure out what is the truth and what is Marilyn's perception of the situation.)

In her own words, "I had—let's see—ten, no, eleven families. The first one lived in a small town near Los Angeles—I was born in Los Angeles. I stayed with them until I was around seven. They were terribly strict. They brought me up harshly, and corrected me in a way I think they never should have—with a leather strap. That finally came out, and so I was taken away and given to an English couple. Life with them was pretty casual and tumultuous."

As a child Marilyn developed a bad stutter that continued to adulthood. "In the orphanage I began to stutter. The day they brought me there, after they pulled me in, crying and screaming, suddenly there I was in the large dining room with a hundred kids sitting there eating, and they were all staring at me. So I stopped crying right away. Maybe that's a reason along with the rest: my mother and the idea of being an orphan. Anyway, I stuttered."

REVISIONIST HISTORY. WAY REVISIONIST HISTORY

All people, celebrities especially, recraft their personal stories to one degree or another.[4] Jackie came by this instinct naturally. At the time of her marriage to JFK, her Bouvier relatives spun the fanciful story that they were descended from Charlemagne and were vastly superior to the bootleggin', knockabout, who-knows-where-the-money-came-from Kennedys. "It was a fairy

4 See Madonna, who somehow ended up with a posh English accent by way of Rochester Hills, Michigan.

tale history," said her cousin John Davis. They were actually descended from a French cabinetmaker named Michel Bouvier who came to America in 1815 and settled in Philadelphia.

Jackie's great-grandfather, Dr. James Lee, was a superintendent of the New York City public school system, although Janet Bouvier preferred to tell people that he was a Maryland-born veteran of the U.S. Civil War and peripherally related to Robert E. Lee. By the end of her life, she came to believe this was actually true and wondered why her name was not included in official genealogies of the Lee family.

Now, in thinking about your own background and wondering where it fits into the Jackie or Marilyn scenario—

Did you have a truly crazy childhood? And not just "My parents didn't buy me a BMW on my sixteenth birthday"? We mean Oprah Bad. Chances are you are a Marilyn.

Did it propel you to "make" something of yourself, almost to the exclusion of all else? Again, Marilyn.

At the other end of the spectrum, do you feel the urge to take your family's history—which is fine the way it is, really—and with a nip and tuck here, a bit of polish there, make it even better? Then you are a Jackie.

In this age of Google, it is difficult, if not impossible, to pretend to go to Harvard or Spence when you did not, but cast off those nutty cousins or aunts and uncles! Forget those Irish forebears in favor of French aristocracy (much chicer, anyway)! Bag Catholicism and join the Episcopal Church!

Like Jackie, you can choose to be above it all. Ignore the haters. Admit nothing. Work behind the scenes with a family flunky (in her case, Mary Van Rensselaer Thayer) and have her ghostwrite your biography while you are in the White House, as Jackie did. (Unknown to the public at the time, Thayer "wrote" *Jacqueline Bouvier Kennedy*, "a warm, personal story of the First Lady illustrated with family pictures" with a strong editorial assist from Mrs. K, who gave her pages and pages of handwritten notes on yellow legal paper.)

Toward the end of your life, when you are truly famous because of your own accomplishments, embrace your formerly spurned ethnic heritage in a big way. Jackie made a point of watching the Saint Patrick's Day Parade from her Fifth Avenue balcony, and JFK Junior had a shamrock tattooed on his backside.

Marilyn, on the other hand, had none of the lyrical childhood memories of Jackie to look back on and enjoy . . . books, her own horse, the rose gardens at Lasata. Instead, she escaped to the movies at Grauman's Chinese Theatre or looked out her window at the water tower of RKO Pictures and dreamed of someday being a star.

"The world around me then was kind of grim," she recalled. "I had to learn to pretend in order to . . . I don't know . . . block the grimness. The whole world seemed sort of closed to me. . . . (I felt) on the outside of everything, and all I could do was to dream up any kind of pretend-game."

SHOULD YOU PLAY THE DAMSEL IN DISTRESS?

No matter what Jackie's upbringing was like (her mother had a fierce temper—"high strung" in yesterday's kinder parlance—and used to slap her or hit her with a hairbrush when she was frustrated.[5] "Nothing we ever did was good enough," recalled Jackie's younger sister, Lee.), there was no way she was going to complain about it to anyone. Ever. She just wasn't built that way.

Marilyn's childhood, on the other hand, was tragic. Perhaps

---

5 In one memorable incident, she threw a knife at a maid for not folding towels properly.

because of her unstable upbringing, Marilyn often felt alone, uncared for. During times of stress or pressure, she felt (rightly or wrongly) that she was alone in the world, without anyone to help her or rely upon. In speaking with journalists, lovers, psychiatrists or close friends, she would talk about her childhood, about what had happened to her in the past, and change the details of the stories around just a bit. Was she really raped at the age of eleven? Did she have sixteen abortions? Was she forced to subsist on $1 a day (and take acting classes) as a struggling starlet? Was she a streetwalker on Hollywood Boulevard?

And finally, did the facts of her story matter so much as the essential truth she told—and believed—herself? As a friend of hers noted, "Marilyn had the talent to make people feel sorry for her and she exploited it. Even people who had been around and around and around, they fell for this: help me."

This vulnerability and the need to shade her life story (depending on who she was speaking with) also became an essential part of the Marilyn myth.

J+M FIELD NOTES: DECIDE WHO YOU WANT TO BE

"I'm going to be a great movie star some day."

—MM

. . . .

"I could be a sort of Overall Art Director of the Twentieth Century, watching everything from a chair landing in space. . . ."

—JKO

While Marilyn's early rise in Hollywood was not swift, once she saw how much she loved being in front of a camera, she had found her beacon, her calling. She was tenacious. She saw a path. She moved to Hollywood, divorced her first husband, took acting lessons, dyed her hair blonder and blonder to emulate her favorite, Jean Harlow. She went on auditions, dieted ruthlessly, lived on a dollar a day and posed for practically any photographer who asked.

She got around, freshening drinks and clearing ashtrays at studio president Joe Schenck's Sunday-night poker parties. She got a contract at 20th Century Fox for $126 a week.

Even before they hit their stride, Jackie and Marilyn both presented themselves to the world in the way they wanted to be perceived—Marilyn as a Hollywood movie star and Jackie . . . well, she did not know exactly what she wanted to be (in later years, she said that she might have liked to be a writer or a journalist, before her life took a different path), but she wanted to get out there and lead an interesting life.

At the risk of getting too metaphysical, the first secret in discovering your essential Jackie-ness or Marilyn-ness is to *de-cide* who you want to be, and then move forward from there. This ability to "know yourself" does not just work for being more like Marilyn or Jackie; it can be applied to any creative field you want to be successful in—from Wall Street or politics to the fashion biz.

THE JACKIE, THE MARILYN: JUDGING CHARACTER

Jackie—or the Jackie-esque Gal—adores history, the telling story or anecdote that reveals character. She is drawn to the great man (or woman, but more likely the man), to her possible place in the scheme of things and how she might be part of something greater than herself. Politics interest her in the purely Shakespearean sense—the characters involved, the actions they take, or don't, when they think no one is looking.

Jackie believes that adversity reveals character. She abhors weak men, people who complain (*Get on with it!* she practically wants to shake them[6]), as well as bullies, fatties, those

. . . .
6 But doesn't.

without style (or those with a masculine style that reveals itself in wide lapels and goofy ties). She really doesn't like high-pitched voices—in men or women.

Out in the real world, she loves four-year-olds but is very suspicious of grown men who dress like them (a baseball cap, cargo shorts and T-shirt in the city). If a grown man is wearing clogs, Crocs or running shoes outside of a gym or professional kitchen—well, that says all one needs to know about him, in the Jackie's mind.

For her part, the Marilyn of today is far more understanding of the foibles of human nature. She has seen more of the world—both its glamorous and unseemly side—than her sister in style, the Jackie. She tends to take people and situations as they are: hoping for the best in people, not that surprised when it does not work out. *Que sera sera* and all that.

In this sense, she is far more vulnerable than Jackie.

A PSYCHOLOGICAL TIME-OUT FOR LES GALS

In recasting her childhood, her father, her relationship with her mother and (as we will see) both of her marriages, Jackie was enormously disciplined about looking at her life and seeing it the way she wanted it to be. Perhaps an early proponent of *The Secret,* she once admitted, "I always push unpleasant things out of my head on the theory that if you don't think about them they won't happen."

Marilyn, on the other hand, was psychologically looser. Emotionally, she was all over the map—giddy, glowing, charismatic one moment, then depressed the next. She was much freer with her emotions than Jackie (probably freer than most people in general) and not afraid to show them.

On some level Marilyn must have also known that the ability to do whatever the hell she wanted at any time—and get away with it—was part of what made her attractive to people and was no small part (along with her talent and her beauty) of what made her a star.

Because any true star deserving of her fans is a bit of a diva, isn't she?[7] We expect it of them.

"I'm selfish, impatient and a little insecure," Marilyn once admitted. "I make mistakes, I am out of control and at times hard to handle. But if you can't handle me at my worst, then you sure as hell don't deserve me at my best."[8]

Is one better than the other? In a perfect world, it might be good to be a mixture of both. Psychologists are now learning that it is actually healthier to focus on what you want and ignore what you don't. In fact, opponents of marriage counseling say that focusing on a couple's problems and endlessly talking talking talking talking about them can actually make them worse, rather than leading to any kind of a resolution.

On the other hand—don't you think it would be fun to just blow off steam once in a while and not be so *conscientious* about everything?

7 Liz Taylor, Sharon Stone in her heyday, Winona Ryder, Mariah Carey . . .
8 Which, you have to admit, is kind of the perfect diva statement.

GOSSIP GIRLS

Although she is often the subject of some speculation in her group (whether she lives in the city or a one-stoplight town), the Jackie of today is Queen Bee in any group and *lives* for gossip.[9] In the midst of society, she appears to float above it, not to care (and on a certain level she doesn't; she has her own thing going on). But on the other hand, there is nothing—nothing—she likes better than a tête-à-tête with a girlfriend (or even better, a guy).

Having said all this, the Jackie is wildly discreet, almost to the point of Ice Princess-dom about what is going on in her own life. Possibly because she grew up as the daughter of divorce, possibly because at a very young age, when she confided in the adults in her life, they had a habit of throwing it back at her in a moment of rage, but the Jackie has a lot of secrets.

This is part of what gives her power—her ability to hold people's confidences and not reveal them. And to keep her own. She collects anecdotes and stories about famous people—Pamela Harriman, Hillary Clinton, Keith Richards—and reads thick biographies for insight into how they did it. She likes to learn as much as she can about people—whether in history or real life.

She also knows, if she knows anything, that "discretion is the better part of valor," quoting Falstaff as only a Jackie-esque Gal can.

But what the heck, it works.

And what sort of gossip does the Jackie like? Anything. Everything. But she can't be bothered scrolling the Internet or (god forbid) watching television—too obvious, too public, too known. She likes the really good stuff you hear at dinner parties (dessert has just

9 We're sorry, she does.

been put out, the table of twelve is polishing off its fourth or fifth bottle of wine, and the conversation keeps getting louder and rowdier), that—if printed— would get the *US Weekly* editor tossed in jail. The kind of stuff you can't wait to tell your lunch date the next day, strictly sotto voce.

The Marilyn, on the other hand, does not gossip. She has been on the receiving end too often and heard too many lies, half-truths and innuendos about herself. It's too painful to think about, all the slush swirling around her.[10]

THE J+M QUICKTEST:

To begin to ascertain your essential Jackie-ness or Marilyn-ness, read the following statement and ask yourself: Does this ring true for me right now? For best results, be like Marilyn—don't overthink things, and follow your first instinct.

The Marilyn Quicktest: People give you things. You don't know why.

The Jackie Quicktest: With the exception of your mother, people tend to do what you say. You don't push it.

10 Oh and BTW, the Jackie Gal has no compunction about gossiping about the Marilyn. None whatsoever. She figures: It's a tough world out there.

FACE IT: SECRETS = MYSTERY

You can look at it any way you want, but both Jackie and Marilyn were women of mystery even at a very young age, because they had a lot to hide. And in this age of the twenty-four-hour news cycle, the ubiquitous Internet, and bloggers intent on sharing Every. Little. Thing, keeping one or two secrets of your own can be sort of empowering.

Think of it—why is Don Draper so darn seductive? Secrets. (Like, a *lot* of them.) And who cares if it is causing him great internal struggle and tearing him up inside (well, this season anyway)—he looks fantastic! Daniel Craig as James Bond? Secrets. Angelina Jolie? Secrets!

And why is someone like Heidi Pratt so blessedly uninteresting? No secrets.

KEEPING TO YOURSELF = MYSTERY

Marilyn's grade-school science teacher, Mrs. Nash, remembers her as being "a good child, but a little set apart." After her parents' vituperative divorce (that went on for four years and remained an ongoing skirmish for the rest of Jack Bouvier's life), Jackie withdrew into herself. As early as high school, Jackie was known among her schoolmates for being self-contained and keeping her own counsel. At Vassar, she studied hard but disappeared most weekends.

MYSTERY = MYSTERY

And finally, don't give away the ball game. While Marilyn might *appear* nude onscreen in her conversation-stopping, flesh-colored tulle and satin evening gowns (in *Bus Stop,* for example), she was never actually unclothed. It was the 1950s, after all, and Marilyn knew how to work the striptease of what is shown and not shown to her advantage.

Same thing with Jackie. Once she had been admitted into

the rambunctious, wily, competitive inner sanctum of the Kennedy dining room early in her marriage, JFK turned to her and said, "A penny for your thoughts."

"But they're my thoughts," she responded. "And they wouldn't be my thoughts anymore if I told them, now would they?"

Touché.

SECRET SECRETS—THE JACKIE: THINGS YOU MIGHT NOT KNOW ABOUT HER

Whether she admitted it or not, Jackie always wanted to lead a big life. Always. In her high school yearbook, she wrote that one of her ambitions was "to not be a housewife."

SECRET SECRETS—THE MARILYN: THINGS YOU MIGHT NOT KNOW ABOUT HER

In school, Marilyn's favorite subjects were English and art. "I hated math, and numbers. . . . I would just stare out the window and daydream."

2 Emulating Jackie Style and Marilyn Style

"I never leave my house unless I'm suitably dressed."

—JKO

. . . .

"I don't know who invented high heels, but all women owe him a lot."

—MM

*I*n terms of style, Jackie and Marilyn are opposite sides of the coin—light and dark. Day and night. Acceptability and sex. Sophistication and playful naïveté.

If Jackie was French couture and the sleeveless shift, Marilyn was the white silk dress slipping off her shoulders as she laughed, pretending not to notice.

The intriguing thing about both Jackie's and Marilyn's style is that they knew what worked for them and used this to their advantage. Nothing was an accident. As a young model trying to break into Hollywood, Marilyn soon found out that if she was a blonde, she got more work from photographers. It took her sixteen tries to get the right shade that would transform her from brown to bombshell, but once she was as blonde as Harlow, she never looked back. Shortly thereafter, in true diva mode, she even made a point of surrounding herself with as much white as possible—from the outfits she chose to the furnishings in her apartment.

It is also said that Marilyn shaved one-quarter inch off the right heel of her shoes (always, always heels—never loafers, ballet flats or, god forbid, sneakers) so that she would walk with a bit of an awkward gait, making her hips even more noticeable. And if you think of her opening entrance in *Some Like It Hot*, when she transfixed us (along with Tony Curtis and Jack Lemmon) with her mesmerizing stroll down the station platform, you know that Marilyn knew exactly what she was doing.

> *"I learned to walk as a baby and I haven't had a lesson since."*
>
> —MM

Both Marilyn and Jackie developed their own very distinct visual presentations. With slight modifications, Jackie (like Audrey Hepburn) found a style early on that worked for her and kept it—more or less—for the rest of her life.

And because their style sense was so strong and unique, both Marilyn and Jackie developed identifiable looks that the rest of us, whether we are in the mood to be a classic or a sexpot (or a classic sexpot), have been riffing on ever since.

FOR JACKIE, FOR MARILYN, FOR YOU: STYLE IS EVERYTHING

When it comes to achieving Jackie or Marilyn mystique, 98 percent of the endeavor hinges on having a signature style—a style that you might actually possess at the moment or one that you aspire to.

Think of someone like Coco Chanel, one of Jackie's favorite designers. No surprise, JKO, like Coco, was also a Leo, and although she always claimed to be wearing Oleg Cassini in the White House, she actually wore a lot of Chanel and Hubert de Givenchy (passed off as American made Cassini). In addition to the material and cut of her suits, Jackie must have admired Chanel's gumption. Chanel's sense of self was so acute, her talent so unquestioned, her ego so vast, that we are still wearing—and coveting—her designs more than half a century later.

In fact, Chanel's personal style was so essential to who she was that she founded a fashion empire based entirely on her own whims.

Although they came from opposite sides of the social scale, Jackie and Marilyn shared Chanel's belief that more than a mere dress, style was essential—style defined who you were. In fact, if you were to look at the silhouette of either Jackie or Marilyn (Jackie—classic, Marilyn—fitted to within an inch of her life, and then some), you would be able to tell, instantly, who was who.

THE LOOK

Interestingly, in terms of their style, the looks that "worked" for them were almost polar opposites—MM favored softer, shinier fabrics that clung to her body and celebrated her awe-inspiring curves, while JKO was more tailored. She did not wear revealing styles or fabrics. Jackie's shape was always suggested, not overtly revealed. As a young wife to John F. Kennedy shuttling between the Cape and Georgetown, on the campaign trail and in the White House, and up until the mid-1960s, she favored spare outfits that hid her body. Her bouffant hairdo, boxy sheaths and three-quarter-inch heels were very much a public uniform, hiding the woman within.

Once Jackie shed her state wear (and the baggage and expectations that went along with being the wife of a president), she looked decades younger. A photographer friend who took her picture in the 1970s when she was working as an editor at Doubleday thought she looked younger in her fifties than she did while in the White House.

Jackie dressed herself within a certain classic framework but added her own individual twist to reveal her personality, while Marilyn (when not being stupefyingly attractive in capri pants and a simple T-shirt) was pure Hollywood glamour.

 RX—THE JACKIE LOOK

When going for the Jackie, think East Coast sophistication with a soupçon of Paris style and a dash of the tomboy (okay, okay, we'll stop with the Julia Child metaphors). The look is clean, classic, somewhat spare without being minimal or overly Comme des Garçons. Very American. As shorthand, we might say Ralph Lauren, except that (as a Jackie) you know that RL is aping *your* style.

That said, there are a few rules in acquiring Jackie Style.

You wear your clothing; your clothing never wears you.

This is a hard thing to teach,[1] but it has to do with being comfortable in your own skin. This is why JKO (or someone like Audrey Hepburn or even Elvis Pres-

---

1 As a Jackie, we know you know it already!

ley) never used or needed a stylist. Through trial and (very little) error, she knew what worked for her.

You know when you see an actress or singer on the red carpet and she looks really uncomfortable, like she's playing dress-up or wearing a costume? Well, that's not what you want. Ideally, as a Jackie, your style will be a reflection of your life, your experiences, your (dare we say) background. It's also why you want to nab well-made pieces from your mom, dad, grandfather, one of your brothers, your current boyfriend. Not only is the older stuff generally better made, but it's your history—wear it!

Make sure your clothing fits you.

We cannot stress this enough. If you do nothing else, make sure your damn clothing fits! (Please, no trousers puddling on the floor or jacket cuffs that are too long.) It takes minutes to go to a tailor and have everything fitted at the waist, the hemline, the cuff.

Get the best stuff you can afford.

To be honest, we're not wild about buying tons and tons of cheap clothing. Well, maybe a piece or two every few years from H&M, but even then, it's sort of a goof, right? As a Jackie, you are going to shop more like the French or a *Vogue* editor—know what you want, buy the best stuff you can afford, take care of it, wear the heck out of it, and at the end of your life, either leave it to the Costume Institute (á la couture goddess Nan Kempner[2]) or your fortunate nieces.

Besides, here's something we learned from the men

2 Who was so insane about couture that she basically kicked her own children out of her NYC apartment and converted their bedrooms into several walk-in closets for herself.

in our lives who have their suits "built" (as they say) on Savile Row—we know of no other incentive to keep your waistline in shape than buying good clothing. As an added benefit, you will also hang it up properly and not drop it on the floor.

Keep it loose.

This is a hard thing to impart, but once you have decent clothing, wear it lightly. Don't wear a single designer all at once. Don't wear anything that screams label label label. Mix the high and the low—jeans and a pair of Vivier shoes. The main thing is this: You don't want to seem as if you are trying too hard. Wear Schlumberger on the subway (the chances of anyone knowing what it is are pretty much nil, and besides, it's insured). You know you are in the Jackie Zone when you can wear a ball gown or a bathing suit as effortlessly as jeans and a T-shirt (or vice versa).

 JACKIE'S STYLE FAVORITES

Jackie's style favorites were a compendium of high-end European designers mixed in with some classic American sportswear. First, the big boys (or girls): Chanel, Valentino, Givenchy, YSL, Gucci, Giorgio Armani, Carolina Herrera, Hermès handbags. Then, moving on to her more casual, everyday favorites: Lacoste, Lily Pulitzer, Zoran, Roger Vivier buckled flats, Jack Rogers sandals, Manolo Blahnik, Ferragamo, Creed Fleurissimo perfume, Tretorn sneakers, Dunhill cigarette lighter, cotton T-shirts from the Gap, Schlumberger enameled bracelets (pricey!), the occasional jodhpurs worn indoors. And as far as riding in style, she gave a Jaguar as a gift to JFK when he was a senator (and it had to be exchanged for an American car), and in later years she drove a BMW.

And where did Jackie like to shop? Um, anywhere on earth? In New York City, her number-one primo spot was probably Bergdorf Goodman, but she also favored the exclusive emporiums on Madison Avenue—Armani, David Webb, Porthault for linen. In Paris, there were the usual suspects—Hermès, Givenchy and Fogal, where she got her stockings.

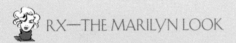 RX—THE MARILYN LOOK

When you're channeling Marilyn, you're asking for the ultimate va va voom and then some. But remember, part of the reason we are still drawn to MM is her combination of sexual knowingness and innocence—and that particular alchemy is important. When making wardrobe choices, the right decision can mean the difference between being in the Marilyn Zone and looking like Pamela Anderson or Anna Nicole Smith.

It's all about the waist.

The basic premise of Marilyn Style is this: No matter your dress size (which, if you know what you are doing in terms of fashion, does not really matter that much), if you have a waist, we want to see it. And that means one thing: Cinch it.

If you are less than thrilled with your figure, take a

tip from the ladies of *Mad Men* and utilize some undergarments that can give you the figure you want.

Show some skin!
· · · · · · · · · · · · ·

Listen—you're gorgeous, you're fabulous in the sack, you love champagne, everyone in the world wants to go out with you—what the heck—own it! If you have legs, we want to see them. If you have gorgeous arms, a beautiful neck, perfect hands . . . you get the idea. The Marilyn is never afraid to show some skin. What she doesn't want to do is show too much of it—no belly button (unless she is—lucky world—wearing a bikini). No tramp stamp.

Have a sense of humor.
· · · · · · · · · · · · · ·

And again, as we said with Jackie, the best thing about Marilyn Style is that you don't have to take it (or yourself) too seriously. As a Marilyn Gal, you won't—this is part of your appeal, after all. Men (and many women and children and dogs) especially hate it when it seems as if someone is trying too hard. So you can be on a first date. You can be walking the red carpet or dripping in diamonds (borrowed from Winston, natch), but it's always good to take yourself lightly.

MARILYN'S STYLE FAVORITES

Marilyn's style was more eclectic than Jackie's. Rather than automatically falling into the classic column, she was a Hollywood starlet who reveled in being photographed. Hence, she took more risks with skintight satin, bright colors, strategically placed bows and polka dots, plunging halter dresses, dangling rhinestone earrings, white fur wraps, peep-toe shoes and some serious (god-given) décolletage.

Like most modern American women, Marilyn mixed casual sportswear with some pricey, one-of-a-kind showstoppers. Although she did not have a ton of clothing for a celebrity of her stature (especially compared to the übershopper Jackie), she took her pieces and, by the very fact that she was wearing them, made them her own. She tended to wear her clothing a good deal and then duck into the wardrobe room at Fox if she needed to borrow something for an awards show or a night out at Romanoff's.

When she was not in costume on a movie set, Marilyn wore a lot of pure American sportswear—JAX (also favored by Audrey Hepburn and Patricia Kennedy Lawford), Madcap, Geistex, John Moore and Levi's, Lee or J.C. Penney denim. In terms of designers we might know today, Emilio Pucci was her absolute favorite, as well as Billy Travilla, who designed her iconic white cocktail dress from *Seven Year Itch,* as well as the hot pink gown she wore while singing "Diamonds Are a Girl's Best Friend" in *Gentlemen Prefer Blondes.* Marilyn favored Ferragamo heels (in case you were wondering, those were Ferragamo white slingbacks worn while cavorting over the subway grate in the *Seven Year Itch*). In addition to wearing off-the-rack cocktail dresses, she also had some pricey couture—Norman Norell, Ceil Chapman, Galanos.

When she was in Manhattan, she favored a camel hair coat or a Blackglama mink that was a gift from Joe DiMaggio.

Marilyn did not have much real jewelry—she owned a 16-inch strand of Mikimoto pearls given to her on their honeymoon in Japan (she gave it to the teenaged Susan Strasberg and Strasberg later returned it to Mikimoto in 1998). She had her platinum and diamond eternity wedding band from Joe DiMaggio. (The ring with thirty-five baguette-cut diamonds—one was missing—was later sold at auction for $772,500.)

J+M FIELD NOTES—THE FIVE ESSENTIALS

JACKIE'S FIVE STYLE ESSENTIALS

Sheath dress—Although she didn't wear them much past 1972, the sleeveless sheath dress still worked when Jackie was having a Camelot redux moment, and the sheath still works today (hello, Mrs. Obama!). Some advice? Your arms have to be in very good shape to pull off this look, so don't neglect those push-ups.

White jeans, or navy blue—JKO was one of those lucky women who looked great in boyishly trim jeans (see also Audrey Hepburn, Kate Moss and Amanda Burden) well into her sixties. Must have been all the speed walking she did around the island of Manhattan, trying to escape the long lens of paparazzo Ron Galella. Although she wore blue jeans in her twenties, nothing says upper class like the white jeans she wore later in sunny Greece or Martha's Vineyard.

T-shirt—JKO (like her future daughter-in-law Carolyn Bessette) favored Petit Bateau in white, navy blue or striped. Although you can now pick them up stateside, she got hers by the dozen in Paris.

Killer jewelry—And when we say killer, we mean some killer, *crazy* jewelry—like the gold and ruby ear clips that Jackie's second husband, Greek shipping magnate Aristotle Onassis, got her in 1969 to commemorate man's landing on the moon. They were a literal representation of the lunar landing, complete with gold spaceships and ruby craters. Made especially for Ari by his jeweler in Greece, of course. But beyond the nutty bibelots, he also got her some extremely serious diamonds from Harry Winston and Van Cleef & Arpels.

Hermès scarf—Tie it under your chin, then put your oversized sunglasses on. Everyone will know it is you, but you can still pretend you are going incognito. Also useful after getting your hair done at Kenneth Salon or Thomas Morrissey's.

MARILYN'S FIVE STYLE ESSENTIALS

Since Marilyn was so physically compelling, she could wear pretty much anything and look amazing. Hence, the basic Marilyn style MO is: "If you've got it, flaunt it."

Devastating evening dress—Billy Travilla (known simply as Travilla) created some of MM's most iconographic evening dresses. They first met in 1950, when she asked if she could borrow his fitting room to try on a costume.

They worked together on eight movies—and what movies they were: *Monkey Business* (1952), *Don't Bother to Knock* (1952), *Gentlemen Prefer Blondes* (1953), *How to Marry a Millionaire* (1953), *There's No Business Like Show Business* (1954), *River of No Return* (1954), *The Seven Year Itch* (1955) and *Bus Stop* (1956). He was nominated for an Oscar for his work on two Marilyn movies, *There's No Business Like Show Business* and *Bus Stop*.

Travilla designed most of Marilyn's most memorable costumes and helped to sew her into the sheer gold lamé dress she wore (briefly—it was deemed too revealing to pass the censors) in *Gentlemen Prefer Blondes*.

Not surprisingly, MM recognized his talent, too. Lifelong friends, she autographed a nude calendar for him with the words "Billy Dear, please dress me forever. I love you, Marilyn."

Daytime/cocktail dress—Marilyn had such a great figure that she could rock a white halter dress and look amazing. For daytime, she liked color in casual West Coast styles—Pucci or a lime green dress in a soft silhouette. For night, her preferred color was (no surprise) black in either drapey wool or velvet.

Bikini (oh, what the heck)—The string bikini was not in evidence in Marilyn's day, so hers tended to be fairly high waisted and somewhat prim by today's standards, although they did reveal her belly button. We have never seen a bathing-suit shot of MM where she was not smiling and looking very happy. So the moral is this: If you are going to wear a bikini, make sure you have gotten a pedicure and *own it*.

White terry cloth bathrobe (nude underneath)—For relaxing at home or on set between takes while having your hair/makeup done. It has to be thick white terry cloth, tied closure in front. You can be like a real star and nab yours from the Chateau Marmont or the Beverly Hills Hotel.

Beautiful silk slip with lace inserts—This can also double as negligee. (We know that the Marilyn doesn't actually wear a nightgown.)

A fashion time-out from *Mad Men*'s Joan Holloway that Jackie or Marilyn would agree with: "Make sure your slip shows just a tiny, tiny bit when you're sitting down because that's alluring."

FOR MM A HEEL. ALWAYS.

Herewith some advice based on Marilyn's shoe collection. For starters, the shoe, and the foot itself, cannot be underestimated in Marilyn World. (Fashion strivers, fetishists and Louboutin wannabes, take from that what you will.)

The heel (much like the red-toed pedicure) is so vital in and of itself to the Marilyn psyche that were the Marilyn Gal ever to write her autobiography (and what the heck, we are sure she will be asked), it would probably be titled *A Heel. Always.*

MM wore Ferragamos, although if she were here today, she would no doubt be wearing Manolo, Louboutin or Jimmy Choo. Jackie wore Blahniks when they were very much the insider's shoe—you could only get them at one shop off King's Road in London and then in one tiny shop in NYC.[3]

What shoes would they wear? Marilyn had more leeway in terms of style. Unlike Jackie, she *always* wore heels. Her shoes (for lack of a better term) were sexier—she might wear peep-toe stilettos or rope-heeled espadrilles with a striped shirt and a little pair of shorts, T-straps, even cowboy boots.

TO FUR OR NOT TO FUR

Let's tackle the animal rights question. How would Jackie and Marilyn come down on this one?

To begin, we have to say that when they were both alive (right up until the early 1990s), wearing a fur was a badge of success, a sign that you had made it (and in a lot of places, it still is). Wearing a fur was also a decidedly romantic gesture—since a spouse or admirer had often given the pricey fur as a gift.

Plus, Marilyn is the (and we mean *the*) iconic blonde in a dark mink.

On the other side of the argument is the fact that Jackie and Marilyn were devoted animal lovers. They both had dogs as pets,

. . . .

3 As a bachelor, JFK Junior was known to go to the Manhattan shop with a page torn out of *Vogue* and buy shoes for his current girlfriend.

while Jackie owned several horses throughout her life, and her children owned goldfish, hamsters, etc. After JKO wore a leopard-skin coat as first lady (a gift from the emperor of Ethiopia), so many were killed by Jackie wannabes trying to copy her that they almost became extinct, and this did not make her happy.

So they would probably be pro–animal rights in theory.

But on the other hand, Jackie and Marilyn were each extremely individualistic free thinkers who did exactly what they wanted, regardless of what others thought they should do.

So, fur? No fur? They both certainly owned and wore a lot of fur during their lifetimes.[4] Were Jackie or Marilyn alive today, our instinct is that they would have come down on the side of individual rights and done whatever they felt like.

MM AND JEANS

Marilyn *owned* denim.

And while Jackie looked cute in jeans (particularly cropped white jeans in the summer), she didn't cause people to stop dead in their tracks when she walked by, and people aren't still discussing how great her, ahem, figure looked in them.

Marilyn's jeans were so iconic that when they were auctioned off by Christie's, New York, in 1999, designer Tommy Hilfiger bought three pairs worn in her 1954 movie *River of No Return* for $42,550.[5]

At the same sale, he also bought her boots from 1961's *The Misfits* for $85,000.

He gave one pair of MM's jeans to Britney Spears and another to Naomi Campbell as gifts. And if you are ever fortunate enough to visit him, he has one pair enshrined in his office.

. . . .

4 MM, in particular, owned several mink coats, a fox stole, rabbit muffs . . . all kinds of fur. And you know what? Who knows what she would choose to do if she were alive today (probably follow the Stella McCartney route), but she wore it well.
5 The inside tag reads "J.C. Penney 24 waist"

THE MARILYN RX—CARING FOR YOUR JEANS

Here is the skinny on caring for your jeans.

Unless you are out mucking around in the mud or work in a coal mine, you don't need to wash your jeans all that often; depending on how often you wear a particular pair, once or twice a month should be enough.

Fashion experts believe that jeans, worn correctly, are as revealing of your identity as a fingerprint. To that end they advise—no kidding—that you should not wash your new jeans for at least six months. Or longer. Unless you are a college freshman or in a rock band,[6] we don't know how realistic this is, so we advise a happy medium . . . wear your jeans for as long as you can before washing them.

If you are trying to keep your jeans dark (much chicer), turn them inside out before tossing them into the washing machine. And separate your light and your dark clothing before washing so your favorite white T-shirts don't turn light blue.

If your jeans fit perfectly, turn them inside out and wash them in cold water so they keep the same shape and the color doesn't run. Personally, we like to wash our jeans in warm or even hot water if we are trying to shrink them a bit.

Finally, the dryer. Some denim fashionistas advise that you take your newly washed jeans, put them on and (we kid you not) sit in a bathtub filled with water for a while so the denim will mold to your shape. They then (and this is the truly insane pièce de résistance) suggest that you walk around in your wet denim until you have a perfect fit.

Wow.

We love our jeans, and we love to be fashionable (sort of), but this is beyond the pale, even for us. So please, no—unless you want to court walking pneumonia (*very* un-Jackie or Marilyn), don't do this. Use the dryer.

And finally, never send your jeans to the dry cleaner (where

. . . .

6 Or, you know, you have to go out and interact with other human beings.

they will give them the dreaded center crease) unless you are a European investment banker or a German aristo.

MARILYN MONROE: STUNNING IN A POTATO SACK

Let's put it this way: There is a reason she was a world-famous movie star and one of the most recognized women to this day.

Do you know that phrase "She would look good even in a potato sack?" (Okay, maybe not, it's an oldie, but ask your parents or grandparents.) In 1952, the publicity department at 20th Century Fox decided to make a fringed minidress out of an Idaho potato burlap sack and put the twenty-six-year-old Marilyn Monroe in it. Predictably, the results were stunning. With her Monroe-perfect hair, glorious smile and T-strap sandals, Marilyn looked as glamorous as if she were wearing a Patou gown.[7]

JACKIE KENNEDY: EVERYONE'S FAVORITE DEB

When she made her society debut in 1947, Hearst columnist Igor Cassini dubbed her "Debutante of the Year." By the time her daughter, Caroline, came of age, Caroline refused to even consider being presented to society. And as for Caroline's daughters coming out? Forget it.

QUICKTESTS
. . . .

The Marilyn Quicktest: You never have a bad hair day. Ever. Plus, you look pretty amazing in anything you wear.

The Jackie Quicktest: Sunglasses, day or night: non-negotiable.

. . . .

7 For some reason, celebrity fitness expert Denise Austin re-created this same look to promote the Idaho Potato Commission in 2005. Let's just say there is only one Marilyn.

WAS MARILYN A SIZE 16?

In a word, no. But for some reason, women today are obsessed with Marilyn's weight and dress size. Back in the day, they were obsessed with her shape more than her size, because she was so curvaceous.

For the record, MM was 5 feet 5.5 inches and throughout her life weighed between 116 and 140 pounds (during the Joe DiMaggio years, when she was eating lots of Italian food and had several pregnancies that were not brought to term).[8] Her measurements were 36-23-35.

Without seeing her clothing in person, determining her size by today's standards is difficult. For starters, all of her costumes were custom designed and fitted for her specifically. Having seen her dress dummy, Marilyn had a very narrow back and rib cage, with a bust size of 36C. What made her figure so extraordinary was the 13-inch difference between her bust and hips and her waist, which resulted in an extreme hourglass shape. (Think of the cartoon character Jessica Rabbit, but entirely natural.)

According to designer Jeffrey Banks, "Sizing in the 1950s was much more generous than today. It was not until about 1967 that Anne Klein starting sizing to flatter women—what would have been a 12 in the 1950s was now an 8." In today's world, Jeffrey thinks that MM would have nominally been a size 10 (and with a 23-inch waist, clothing would have seriously been taken in at the midsection), going to perhaps a 12, but with alterations.

So don't kid yourself. Marilyn was a physically compelling woman. While she wasn't the boyishly skinny runway model that seems to pass for beautiful today,

8 At her death in 1962 (at the age of thirty-six), she weighed 117 pounds.

she certainly had (and still does have) her own appeal and millions of fans. There is a reason she was a movie star, perhaps one of the greatest icons (and certainly one of the sexiest) of the 20th century.

JACKIE AS MATERIAL GIRL

We have to hand it to Jackie. When it came to shopping, she was world class.

As one Ari associate described her (and not in a good way), she was "a speed shopper. She could be in and out of any store in 10 minutes or less, having run through $100,000 or more." Truman Capote once recalled accompanying her on "one of those shop-till-you-drop sprees. She would walk into a store, order two dozen silk blouses in different shades, give them an address and walk out." Once she bought two hundred pairs of shoes in a single foray, running up a tab of $60,000.

Part of Jackie's rationale might have been that she was married to one of the richest men in the world, so she should be able to do what she wanted, right? Plus, it helped Onassis's business mystique to be married to one of the most glamorous women in the world, so she couldn't exactly shlub around. Jackie never cut down on her shopping; she simply had the bills sent directly to Ari, or raised cash by selling her clothes—many never worn—on consignment to New York City thrift shops, such as Michael's or Encore.

And she kept right on shopping.

IF JACKIE AND MARILYN
WENT SHOPPING TODAY

JKO:

Michael Kors
Lisa Perry (post-1967)
The Town Shop or Le Petite Coquette for lingerie
J.Crew
Bergdorf Goodman
Lanvin
Charvet, Paris (for the lucky man in her life)
Roger Vivier (NYC outpost on Madison only)
JKO would stop by Red Mango for dessert while
   shopping
Tory Burch
D. Porthault
Jason Wu
Petit Bateau
Van Cleef & Arpels
MIHO flowers (under the premise: It is better to re-
   ceive, than to give.)

MM:

Juel Park Lingerie (Los Angeles—MM had lingerie
   made there, still in business)
MM would completely, *completely*, rock out the DVF
   wrap dress
MM would wear a *Paris Review* T-shirt and drive all
   the lit boys mad. (Available only online. They run
   very small, so order accordingly.)
La Petite Coquette
J. Mendel, Paris
Barneys New York
Oscar de la Renta for big events
Harry Winston
Camel hair coat from Brooks Brothers

They would both nab shirts/cashmere/blazers from
their husband's/boyfriend's closet

SECRET SECRETS — THE JACKIE:
THINGS YOU MIGHT NOT KNOW ABOUT HER

Although she had a wardrobe to rival the second floor of Bergdorf's (and the designer duds to prove it), Jackie wore jeans and a T-shirt 90 percent of the time.

SECRET SECRETS — THE MARILYN:
THINGS YOU MIGHT NOT KNOW ABOUT HER

Although known for her glamorous image, MM disliked wearing makeup or jewelry, wearing little of either in her off hours.

3 *Cultivating Beauty*

"I want to feel blonde all over."
—MM, WHEN ASKED WHY SHE STAYED
PALE AND DID NOT SUNBATHE

. . . .

"I am a woman above everything else."
—JKO

*B*oth Marilyn and Jackie understood the power of beauty. And yet curiously (but perhaps not so surprisingly), neither thought she was pretty growing up. In Jackie's family, her sister, Lee, was considered the "pretty one," while Jackie was considered the "brains."[1]

For better or worse, Marilyn *was* her beauty, was sex. This was both empowering—the control she had over men—but also debilitating because, Jesus, what would happen when she lost her looks or wanted to be taken seriously as something other than a sex object?

A child of Hollywood, Marilyn knew the transience of physical beauty—and in her world, its absolute necessity. "Gravity

. . . .

1 This was similar to the dynamics of Grace Kelly and her family, where her older sister, Peggy, was considered the "star," and Grace (if it can be imagined) the plain Jane. Continuing this theme, Audrey Hepburn (unbelievably) also thought that she was "funny" looking.

catches up with all of us," she said. And this, perhaps, is why it was even more important for her to leave something of lasting value—her own image on the screen.

In terms of their individual beauty, Jackie and Marilyn were almost opposite archetypes—Marilyn lush and light, Jackie darker and more angular. While Marilyn wore Chanel No. 5 perfume to bed, Jackie wore Chanel suits to White House functions. They each made the most of what they had—as a child, Jackie's face was so broad that she had to have her glasses custom made. As the first lady, millions of women around the world copied her style, as she brought the look of French couture from the runways to suburban housewives. Marilyn brought a sense of humor to relations between the sexes, avoided the sun, preferred her clothing skintight, and didn't like to wear underwear.

And each, in her own way, became a style icon.

"BEAUTY IS TRUTH, TRUTH BEAUTY. . . ."

No matter how they chose to present themselves to the world (Jackie in white jeans, T-shirt and Jack Rogers sandals, stepping off a boat in Greece; Marilyn in full movie star regalia—white silk shantung gown and matching fur stole, dripping in diamonds on the red carpet), Jackie and Marilyn were both keenly aware of how they looked and how they appeared in public. Both were great dressers with natural style whether by way of Southampton or Hollywood. Both had an innate aesthetic sense honed from pedigree, interest or necessity.

It may have looked carefree—Marilyn grinning beneath a sheet, being photographed for *Vogue,* Jackie wearing a thin sweater and jeans on a city street, turning to smile for the camera. But don't kid yourself; Jackie and Marilyn took care of themselves. Yes, they were both extremely fortunate in the genetic lottery, but they also pampered their skin, hair and bodies as much as their respective budgets allowed.

JACKIE: TAILORED PERFECTION

As the daughter of Jack Bouvier, a debutante, a Vassar girl, first lady, the wife of a rich man (on two separate occasions), the "most famous woman in the world," Jackie was expected to keep it together. There was no way you would ever see her slouching off to the supermarket in a velour sweat suit with lettering on her backside. Or (god forbid) wearing flip-flops on a city sidewalk. Or with stringy hair. Like the Kennedy women of their generation, the Bouvier gals—Jackie and Lee—were fierce dieters. If Jackie gained as little as 4 pounds, her mother (no slouch in the slim department herself) let her know she had noticed.

MARILYN: BEAUTY WAS SEX

Marilyn's beauty was, literally, her ticket out of a miserable anonymous existence—the kind she had seen her mother endure. Making her way up the Hollywood ladder without a protector, without family connections or the liberal arts education that Jackie had enjoyed, Marilyn almost had to be beautiful to make her way to the head of the line; to get the hell out of where she came from. And even with her considerable physical assets, Marilyn studied her features and highlighted them to give herself even more of an advantage. With Marilyn, nothing was left to chance. When it came to her own self-presentation, she (like Jackie in her own way) was a perfectionist.

Photographer David Conover, who "discovered" Marilyn during an early photo session, said that he could not remember another model "so self critical," nor one who so acutely scrutinized every contact sheet, every negative and print for the tiniest flaw: "What's happened to me here?" she asked, or "This is awful, where did I go wrong?"

It took her one and a half to three hours to turn herself into "Marilyn," which was one of the reasons she was so chronically late for a film set, a meeting or even a cocktail party.[2] She wanted to be perfect. She knew what her audience expected from her (a look that she herself created), and she worked to give it to them. She had to, because she believed that "If I'm a star, then the people made me a star."

. . . .

JKO AND MM SKIN CARE SECRETS

. . . .

As a young woman, Jackie cornered Hollywood starlet Zsa Zsa Gabor on a plane coming back from London (where she had covered Queen Elizabeth's coronation for *The Washington Times-Herald*) to ask about her skin care secrets. Gabor clued her in to Erno Laszlo—a Hollywood skin care specialist little known to the general public whose products were used by Marilyn Monroe, Audrey Hepburn and Ava Gardner, among others. JKO got on the Laszlo bandwagon, too. (Zsa Zsa Gabor also, oddly, advised Jackie to "eat a piece of raw green pepper every single day in order to achieve and maintain beautiful skin." There is no word as to whether JKO ever actually tried this.)

Laszlo's system, still available today, was famously complex, involving many stages—skin was "clocked" depending on level of dryness or oiliness, then there was a whole system of sea mud soap, thirty splashes of lukewarm water, Active pH-elityl Oil, astringent with white powder mixed in for overnight, a different-colored astringent for daytime, various moisturizers for day or night, a loose powder to go over it all. . . .

But both Marilyn and Jackie swore by his methodology.

FIELD NOTES: THE DIET PLAN

Marilyn loved food, and she particularly loved to drink champagne—any time of the day or night. "Just give me champagne and good food and I'm in heaven and love," she said. To

. . . .

2 This did not include hours spent in the bath or her habit of washing and rewashing her hair if she was unhappy with the way it looked.

loosen her up for a memorable 1962 *Vogue* photo shoot, Bert Stern had a case of Dom Pérignon delivered to their bungalow at the Hotel Bel-Air.

And boy, did it work. By the middle of the shoot, Marilyn had shed all of her clothing and was frolicking beneath the white sheets of a rumpled bed, her white-blonde hair blending into the pillow, smiling slyly at the camera, her lips a riotous red, one beautiful bare arm revealed.

Jackie, on the other hand, was fastidious about her weight, her diet, how she looked in clothes, how she appeared in public—there was no *way* she would ever end up nude at the Bel-Air with a case of champagne and Bert Stern shooting away for *Vogue*.

To deal with stress, Jackie smoked two packs of cigarettes a day her entire life, starting from the age of fifteen, and bit her nails to the quick (the yellowing of her fingertips and her nail-biting habit were part of the reason she wore gloves in public, thereby starting a fashion trend). When in the White House, if she felt she had gotten above her goal weight of 120 pounds, she subsisted on little more than broth and fruit for a day or so until she got it down. (For his part, JFK fretted about his midlife weight gain, taking Metamucil before meals in a 1960s-inspired way to lose weight, and he was self-conscious about his "jowls"—worried that no one would vote for him in the next election.)

It continued to the next generation. When their daughter, Caroline, was a teenager and having lunch with her mother at the Ritz in Boston, Jackie delivered the ultimate mom put-down—"You'd better not have dessert, because you'll get fat and no man will want you."

Ouch.

. . . .

THE BOMBSHELL DIET

. . . .

Perhaps because she came of age in the middle of the 20th century, Marilyn's diet was, well, pretty 1950s. The way she ate reflected the most advanced thinking at the time (mainly veggies and protein, avoiding carbs), but it was also grounded in much of the same sound advice we might follow today.

As a struggling actress, Marilyn was poor, often subsisting on a dollar a day (granted, that was in 1940s money), on things like raw hamburger, peanut butter, hot dogs, chili, crackers, oatmeal and orange juice.

A neglected child of the Depression, Marilyn was not a foodie. When she cooked, she kept things very simple . . . and by simple, we don't mean an egg white omelet or skim cappuccino, we mean cooking peas and carrots together because she liked the color combination. At the age of twenty-six, she spoke of her "bizarre eating habits" in a magazine interview (accompanied by a stunning photograph of her in bed with full hair and makeup, seemingly nude beneath a sheet—risqué!— smiling gloriously at the camera), saying that for breakfast she warmed a cup of milk on a hot plate in her hotel room, broke two raw eggs into it, whipped it up with a fork, and drank it while she dressed. And then she had a multivitamin.

During the day she went to acting class, or auditions, or maybe over to the studio lot to see if she could scare up some work as an extra. Occasionally she would stop off at Wil Wright's ice cream parlor for a hot fudge sundae on the way home (interestingly, Audrey Hepburn used to do the same thing in the afternoons). "I'm sure that I couldn't allow myself this indulgence were it not that my normal diet is composed almost totally of protein foods."

"My dinners at home," she said, "are startlingly simple. Every night I stop at the market near my hotel and pick up a steak, lamb chops or some liver, which I broil in the electric oven in my room. I usually eat four or five raw carrots with my meat, and that is all. I must be part rabbit; I never get bored with raw carrots."

Later on in life, even after she had had success, Marilyn still kept things fairly basic. Joe DiMaggio exposed her to Italian food, and after their marriage, she ate pasta on and off for the rest of her life. When married to Arthur Miller, she also tried her hand at Jewish food.

When she wasn't dieting for a film role, she enjoyed hot dogs, caviar, Mexican food, steak (her favorite) and vanilla ice cream (her favorite dessert).

While filming *Let's Make Love* in the late 1950s, she ate a lot of spaghetti and lamb stew, washing it down with vodka and champagne (she considered Dom Pérignon 1953 the best). Like every starlet and socialite of note in the 1950s and '60s (Babe Paley, Jackie Kennedy, legendary *Vogue* editor Diana Vreeland, most people's moms), she often had grapefruit for breakfast (Grace Kelly had hers broiled).

Never heavy by today's standards (where more than half of Americans are overweight), Marilyn's weight generally stayed in the 115- to 120-pound range, although she went up to 140 pounds during her marriage to Joe DiMaggio and her tumultuous years with Arthur Miller, from 1956 to 1961. Although it is difficult to say why she gained so much weight at that time, some theorize that it might have been caused by her three (unsuccessful) pregnancies, the strain of Miller being investigated by the House Un-American Activities Committee, domestic bliss when first settling down with Miller or the strain of the marriage collapsing a few years later.

When she had to lose weight for a role, Marilyn followed what would today be considered the Atkins Diet. A typical breakfast might consist of egg whites poached in safflower oil, toast, hard-boiled eggs or a grapefruit. Lunch might be a broiled steak and some greens. While she cut down on her drinking when she was in "training" (as she put it), she still enjoyed vodka. In 1962 she shed 20 to 25 pounds in preparation for *Something's Got to Give*, and she reported to work thinner and fitter than she had been in years.

. . . .

JACKIE'S TRICKS FOR STAYING SLIM
. . . .

At 5 feet 7 inches Jackie stayed slim through the extremely effective socialite regime of exercise, smoking, and watching what she ate. Oh, and genetics (her sister, Lee, was also exceptionally thin). Having said that, she didn't eat a lot of junk or processed food. There was the occasional chocolate ice cream, but she wasn't rocking it out at McDonald's or anything. She did snack between meals, but it would be sliced carrots or celery sticks.

A MORNING STAPLE: "THE GREEN SMOOTHIE"

Every model, actress and healthy person we know swears by this. Plus, if you are in a hurry, it is an easy way to get your greens. While JFK Junior was a protein shake aficionado, here is an updated recipe Jackie or Marilyn would have followed. It is a great way to start your day.

A green smoothie can be made with any combination of raw greens (lettuce, celery, spinach, kale), water, and some fruit for sweetness (and to make it palatable). If you want it thicker, you can add a few ice cubes at the end. To improve it even more, add a scoop of protein powder and flaxseed.

THE J+M GAL'S GREEN SMOOTHIE

A handful of raw spinach

2 stalks of celery

½ cucumber

Handful of kale (remove stems)

½ apple

1–2 bananas

4–5 frozen whole strawberries

1–2 cups water, depending on thickness

There are a million variations of this smoothie available online. Adding pineapple (canned is fine) is really good. Adding frozen blueberries to *anything* blended is also terrific. Add enough water so it is not too thick.

Make sure you rinse all raw greens to clean them. Frozen fruit (bananas, strawberries, mixed berries) are fine. For best results, you need a strong blender like a Vitamix.

J+M—Food Rules

Here is another question to ponder: What the heck did Jackie and Marilyn eat to look so darn terrific?

For starters, they knew their bodies pretty well, and they knew what they could and could not get away with. Marilyn, for example, knew that if she ate too many croissants or a lot of processed food (Lay's Potato Chips, ice cream—basically, all the fun stuff), the back of her thighs would start looking shlubb-o (at least to her extremely discerning eye).

Jackie, for her part, was almost comically disciplined in terms of what she ate, even more so than Marilyn. By the time she got to the White House, her strict diet was second nature. Not only did she have the knowledge base of a nutritionist, she also kept up to date on the most recent health and medical news (both mainstream and the more outlandish claims) and would have been happy to answer any questions you might have about the importance of getting vitamin D, having some protein for breakfast and how addictive carbs and white sugar can be. After her favorite aunt, Edith Bouvier Beale, and her mother began showing signs of Alzheimer's, she became obsessed with the thought that she might be losing her memory (she wasn't). And she tossed out all the nonstick pans in her kitchen.

> ### Quicktests
> . . . .
>
> **The Jackie Quicktest:** You can actually put down the breadbasket. Like, forever.
>
> **The Marilyn Quicktest:** You might say you are dieting, but really, you like yourself better with curves.

. . . .
JACKIE TODAY: REAL-LIFE ADVICE
. . . .

Don't kid yourself. Although there is an element of genetics involved, the Jackie and Marilyn Gals of today don't look that good without taking care of themselves. They—and particularly the Jackie (who might gleefully eat french fries for lunch but has carrot juice for the rest of the day)—watch what they eat. In real life, Jackie was perfectly capable of surviving on skinless chicken or fish and a lightly dressed salad for dinner. Her regime rivaled that of a Ford model's (well, without the endless coffee and vitamin C powder).

Similarly, if the Jackie-esque gal of today knows she is going to an amazing restaurant that night, she eats lightly during the day. If she spends New Year's Eve at a house party in Gstaad, she makes sure she gets back on the treadmill or the yoga mat when she gets home. You can be certain that when she's in Paris she is going to eat all the croissants she wants—because, after all, isn't France where all the great croissants come from? But she will stay away from carbs once she gets home.

If she is invited to a dinner party or (even better) if a man cooks for her, the Jackie will eat everything on her plate and seconds. If there is homemade dessert—particularly something she does not normally make for herself (Profiteroles! Crème brûlée! Rice Krispies treats!), she is having it.

The real Jackie never turned down an opportunity to have real whipped cream. Ever. She was not a fan of low-fat, pro-

cessed, diet or fake food. When she was on the Vineyard, she made a point of stopping by Mad Martha's Ice Cream shop and having a cone because she knew you needed some fat in your diet to keep your hair and skin looking good.

With her innate sense of what worked for her (as well as an extremely fortunate metabolism), Jackie never got too far off-kilter. And neither does the Jackie Gal of today.

J+M FIELD NOTES: AT THE GYM

Although she looked softer and relatively more fleshy when compared to the angular Jackie, Marilyn was an early proponent of physical exercise. She lifted 5-pound weights during her early years as a young starlet to maintain her bust line and jogged in the morning. Following her masseuse Ralph Robert's instruction, she also took ice baths sprinkled with Chanel No. 5 to highlight her already luminous skin and minimize cellulite.

There was a reason Jackie stayed a perfect size 6 her entire life—she was almost addicted to exercise. She rode horses and also water-skied, jogged, did yoga, went hiking and kayaking and was a member of two health clubs in New York City.[3]

*B*ut what were their particular exercise regimes? For starters, Marilyn would probably have caused a riot if she had shown up at an actual gym the way we would today. She could barely cross the studio lot without men hounding her. But having said that, she was not averse to lifting weights in the privacy of her own home, and when she was just starting out as an aspiring (read: starving) Hollywood starlet, she asked a military instructor who had been a weight-lifting champion to teach her how to use barbells and other gym equipment.

He agreed.

Like Cary Grant, Marilyn put together her own rudimentary workout routine (Grant's home gym was in his garage), which was almost unheard of for a female in the late 1940s, early 1950s. Visitors would find gym equipment in the corner of her living room. At a time when hardly anyone ran for exercise (men or women), she regularly took early-morning jogs through the backstreets of Beverly Hills.

In terms of a regime, here is Marilyn's, in her own words: "Each morning, after I brush my teeth, wash my face and shake off the first deep layer of sleep, I lie down on the floor beside my bed and begin my first exercise. It is a simple bust firming routine using 5-pound weights. . . . I lie on my back and lift my arms as long as I can. I then move the weights in circles until I am tired.

. . . .

3 There was a reason her son, John, looked so good, too. He was a member of four gyms dotted around Manhattan so he could duck in and work out whenever the mood struck. JFK Junior also smoked two cigarettes a day, just to prove that he could.

I don't count rhythmically like the exercise people on the radio. I couldn't stand exercise if I had to feel regimented about it."

And although Marilyn loved romping on Malibu Beach (especially if there was a *LIFE* photographer around) or being out in nature, she was not much for organized sports, such as golf or tennis. "I'll leave those things to the men."

Jackie, on the other hand, was so athletic, she practically could have tried out for the Olympics. Here, the social differences in their upbringing showed. While Jackie's favorite sports were foxhunting, jogging, skiing, flirting, fine dining and competitive shopping, she certainly knew her way around a tennis court and loved sailing, too.

When Jackie was in New York City, she went for a late-morning jog around the Reservoir in Central Park (now renamed after her), occasionally pursued by her nemesis, Ron Galella. Twice a week she used a personal trainer at the Vertical Club on East 56th Street. For the last seventeen years of her life, Tillie Weitzner, a well-regarded yoga instructor, visited her twice a week. When Jackie's non-air-conditioned prewar New York City apartment got overheated, she said that Jackie, wearing "an old black leotard with holes in it," never complained. "Jackie remained very serious about yoga. She was always pushing herself to get better."

During summer months on Martha's Vineyard, Jackie's routine was no less strenuous. After breakfast, mornings were for kayaking, and the hours after lunch might be spent swimming or water-skiing. (During the White House years, Jackie encouraged Joan Kennedy to use flippers when swimming out on the Cape to trim her thighs.)

Fall found Jackie out in Bernardsville, New Jersey, riding horses. She often spent the week before November 22 (the anniversary of JFK's assassination) riding with the Orange Hunt in Middleburg, Virginia, where she stayed at a cottage on Mrs. Paul "Bunny" Mellon's estate.

During the winter—are you still with us?—Jackie was out walking practically every day in Central Park or running errands on Madison Avenue. After Christmas, she recuperated from the holiday hubbub by flying down to Antigua and staying at Curtain Bluff.

. . . .

THE JACKIE RX

. . . .

If you are a Jackie, you are a bit of a jock. You are also more high end when it comes to working out. (And you know that today's Jackie can't just go to any gym—she would have a personal trainer come to her home, or she'd join the Reebok Sports Club in Los Angeles or New York City or the East Bank Club in Chicago.) Plus, the Jackie needs lots of gear— a private lake, a private island with its own security force, yachts, a stable, running shoes, proper riding gear, even a worn leotard.

. . . .

THE MARILYN RX

. . . .

If you are a Marilyn, you're probably a bit more low key, do-it-yourself when it comes to exercise. And really? Unless you are up for a film role or about to shoot a magazine spread, let's be honest—you really don't like exercise anyway. So get some beauty rest (hey, you were probably out late last night), go for a walk on the beach in the late afternoon and lift weights once in a while—*but only if you feel like it.*

Besides, as a Marilyn, you know that it almost doesn't matter what you do in terms of exercise or working out, because you will always—and let's be honest here—*always* be more physically compelling than the Jackie.

JACKIE AND MARILYN: THE EXHIBITIONISTS

"I'm only comfortable when I'm naked," said Marilyn, and given their druthers, the Marilyns of today get out of their skivvies as soon as possible, too. They love being naked. And even fully dressed, they give off the vibe—somehow—of being half dressed.

Marilyn was, if possible, even more beautiful nude than wearing any article of clothing she owned—any bathing suit, sable, jeans, T-shirt, Travilla gown. As her acting teacher Lee Strasberg put it, "Her quality when photographed is almost of a supernatural beauty."

Jackie went topless in public, but only situationally, say, in the south of France or in Greece, where she knew it was very unlikely that she would run into friends of her parents or anyone she knew from the club.

Like many American women even today, Jackie went a little bonkers in Europe. Losing her virginity in an old-fashioned lift in a *pensione* in Paris. ("Is that all there is to it?" she wondered.) Skinny-dipping off Skorpios. Going braless under a T-shirt in the late 1960s. With her puritan forefathers at her back, the Jackie Gal of today will wear beautiful lingerie that costs a week's salary and towering heels overseas—cobblestones be damned!

Today's Marilyn goes much, much further. She has no problem with sex or nudity—she loves her body and feels happiest when she is naked. She also loves taking baths; she loves the water and the beach.

. . . .

PLASTIC SURGERY?
. . . .

In 1950, Marilyn had her nose thinned by a plastic surgeon. Details about the procedure are scarce. Other than that, she seems to have been antisurgery. And she certainly never had breast implants, lip implants, liposuction, Botox, Restylane, or any of the other assists that seem common among most twentysomething starlets (or aspiring Playboy bunnies) today in Southern California. "I want to grow old without face-lifts," she declared. "I want to have the courage to be loyal to the face I have made."

Jackie, on the other hand, had no problem with plastic surgery (as was common with her social set). In the spring of 1989, she had a very subtle face-lift performed by Dr. Michael Hogan, a Park Avenue plastic surgeon.

J+M FIELD NOTES: BODY TYPE

Freud wasn't kidding: Anatomy *is* destiny. Determining whether your body type is more Jackie or more Marilyn, and thus figuring out your attendant decorating, wardrobe, career, spouse and lifestyle choices, it's pretty simple.

In the Jackie/Marilyn worldview, there are only two options: the hourglass or the tomboy. Don't let women's fashion magazines or hectoring "how to dress" cable television shows complicate the issue—it doesn't matter how tall (or short) you are. It doesn't matter what your waist size, your dress size or your shoe size is, or what you weigh when you step on the scale on any given morning. If you have curves, you are a Marilyn, and if not, you are a Jackie.

. . . .

THE MARILYN RX

. . . .

You have curves, so flaunt them. Simple as that. Cinch in that waist. Wear your clothing just a *bit* too small, and cherish the hobble skirt. Get your jeans tailored so that they nip in at the waist (a style-setter trick that the seamstress at your dry cleaner can do for about $10). Better yet, toss your just-washed jeans in the dryer and set it on high so they really shrink. Leave the top three or four buttons on your sweater undone. Don't wear anything underneath said sweater; show some skin. For the Marilyn Gal, a white T-shirt is not a friend.

The basic premise in Marilyn World is that if you can walk

too quickly or too comfortably (or, god forbid, run without twisting your ankle), you are not doing it right. Take it easy. Slow down. Walk away from him and break his heart. Sashay down the Boulevard of Life, and let the world enjoy the view while you are at it.

. . . .

THE JACKIE RX
. . . .

If you have a boyish figure, emphasize that, too. Wear all the things your fuller-figured sisters wish they could (and thereby assuage your guilt at not having to wear a bra when you are home alone). The basic MO is prep with a twist—cropped trousers with no socks. White jeans or corduroy in December. Because your legs are good, set the bar high with a miniskirt. (And if you wear heels, wear tights of a similar shade to continue the line.)

Shop in the boy's department at a place like Brooks Brothers for great quality at a better price. With your straight silhouette, you can be classic with a kick—cowboy boots in the city, a peacoat, sunglasses in the rain, a goofball furry hat (real or faux) picked up at Harvey Nicks in London.

Now, the Jackie Girl—the Jackie Girl strides. No matter what decade she currently occupies, one imagines her, easily, as a nineteen-year-old sophomore dashing across the quad, late for class. Whether in the big city or suburbia, she walks fast as if to outrun the paps (real or imagined) that invariably follow her every move.

THE HAIR GUY—

If conspiracy theorists had their acts together, they would have figured out that hair maestro Kenneth Battelle is the true missing link between Jackie and Marilyn, as he created both of their iconic hairstyles.

In 1954, Kenneth, working at the Helena Rubenstein salon in New York City, made over newlywed Jacqueline Kennedy, softening and lengthening her hair from the Audrey Hepburn in *Roman Holiday* style she previously had.

In 1958, Marilyn, just finishing up *Some Like It Hot,* sought out Kenneth's help on the advice of designer Norman Norell, as her hair was falling out from overbleaching and perming. Kenneth made Marilyn even more *Marilyn* by creating the iconographic blonde goddess hair we associate her with. From then on, she made a point of visiting his salon every time she was in New York. The following year, he traveled with her to Chicago for the world premiere of *Some Like It Hot.*

In 1960, Kenneth created the tousled bouffant for Jacqueline Kennedy, causing something of a stir among old-line socialites (like her mother, Mrs. Auchincloss, who considered it too "casual" and modern looking— and inappropriate).

In 1961, Kenneth did all of the Kennedys' hair for Inauguration Day.

The following year, Kenneth did Marilyn's hair for JFK's forty-fifth birthday rally at Madison Square Garden. A few months later, over the summer, Kenneth styled her hair for what ended up being her final photo session with Bert Stern for *Vogue.* On November 21, 1963, Kenneth cut Jackie's hair at 7:00 a.m., just before she left with her husband for Dallas.

In 1963, Kenneth fulfilled a longtime dream by opening his own salon on East 54th Street, in a 17,000-square-foot townhouse that had been a former Vanderbilt residence. Society decorator Billy Baldwin (a favorite of JKO's) decorated it. For the next thirty years, Kenneth was the go-to guy for society women like Babe Paley, Diana Vreeland, and Happy Rockefeller, as well as styling for *Vogue, Glamour* and *Harper's Bazaar* cover shoots.

Today, Kenneth still works at his salon (now ensconced in the Waldorf) every day. Overseen by artistic director Kevin Lee, it is still flourishing and catering to a new generation of style setters.

THE JACKIE, THE MARILYN HAIR RX

Whether you favor Jackie or Marilyn, your hair is talismanic. Although you don't give it much thought after you brush it in the morning, your hairstyle is so vital to your persona that it almost has its own character. No matter your age, you have the soft hair of a child. If you have it colored—even if it is platinum blonde—you never admit to it.

Of the two, the Jackie is more natural looking. You would never know that she dyes her hair. With the exception of Carmen Dell'Orefice, our favorite model in the entire world, neither the Jackie nor the Marilyn will ever go gray. Ever.

Some of the best advice we've gotten is not to wash it too often. One of the most recent comebacks in beauty tricks is the use of dry shampoo, a very fine powder that was big in the late 1960s. Marilyn got the same effect by sprinkling her roots with Johnson's Baby Powder that had been sifted to give it an even finer consistency. Terrific for travel or when you've gotten your hair done and it has to "last" a few more days. Today, there are even better formulations available.

THE MM LOOK: HOW-TO

We think that if most women had to choose between Jackie Hair and Marilyn Hair, they would choose the latter (if only for the riotous effect it had on the opposite sex).

To get true Marilyn hair, it helps to have Kenneth (New

York) or Gladys Rasmussen (California)—two of Marilyn's longtime hair stylists—on call. But if not, what can today's modern gal do? We spoke with Kevin Lee, artistic director of Kenneth's salon, for advice.

And he said, "To get Marilyn's look, you need a true set. You can get some life with hot rollers on your own, but that really isn't a strong enough hold. You also have to find someone who is talented at setting up a pattern with rollers. Then you have to sit under a hood dryer. Or, you could air dry your hair, but that could take six or seven hours!"

He also advised using setting lotion. But the main thing he said was, "There are modern versions of it. You don't want it to look exactly the way Marilyn's did, but you can tweak it and make it look modern. . . . For Marilyn-type hair—you want it to be touchable, loosened up, because that's what's sexy. You want it almost to look like 'bed head,' the morning after. If it is too stiff or too perfect—that can come off as a little icy."

. . . .
MM: The Evolution of a Blonde
. . . .

While it is commonly perceived that Marilyn's hair was always platinum, her hair actually evolved through the spectrum of blonde possibilities as her career progressed. As a young model just starting out, she was told by Emmeline Snively, owner of the Blue Book Agency, that she would get more work as a blonde, because photographers could work with lighting to change her look. As a young girl, Marilyn also idolized 1930s film star Jean Harlow, and this also fueled her desire for perfect, high-maintenance, almost otherworldly (and really, isn't that the definition of a legendary Hollywood star, too?) platinum blonde.

Marilyn first hit the bottle at Hollywood's Frank Joseph Salon in 1946, where her hair was bleached to a golden blonde and chemically straightened. As her career progressed, she tried out practically every blonde that Clairol invented, among them golden blonde, ash blonde, champagne blonde, honey blonde, bleached blonde, strawberry blonde and platinum blonde, until she reached the apotheosis of pure Marilyn-ness—white blonde. She was also fond of bleaching her pubic hair, as she "liked to feel blonde all over."

By the time she was a world-famous starlet, her hair was so high maintenance that she had to have it highlighted every three weeks to maintain her look. This left her naturally fine hair very brittle and prone to breakage (fortunately, a visit to Kenneth and his magical unguents brought it back to life). By the time of her death in 1962, her hair was completely stripped of pigment to a shade she fondly referred to as "pillow case white."

WHAT YOU CAN TELL FROM A WOMAN'S HANDS

Both the Marilyn and the Jackie Gals of today have beautiful hands that they emphasize by taking care of them, since they know that (even unconsciously) people notice your hands. As first lady, Jackie claimed to use Johnson's Baby Lotion as a moisturizer and later, One & All Hand Cream.

The Jackie wears clear nail polish or a sheer pink color.

Since she uses her hands a lot, she keeps them to a manageable length—no Barbra Streisand talons for her!

The Marilyn will often get away with colored nails—opaque pink to match her evening dress or even red.

SIGNATURE SCENTS

Marilyn Monroe—Chanel No. 5, Fracas, Joy

Jackie—Jicky by Guerlain (also worn by her future daughter-in-law, Carolyn Bessette), Joy, Fleurissimo, Jean Patou 1000

To Tan or Not to Tan?

"Despite its great vogue in California, I don't think sun tanned skin is any more attractive than white skin."

—MM on tanning

JKO was the exact opposite. When we think of Jackie, or any of the Kennedys for that matter, we think of summers on the Cape (or Skorpios) and tan, golden skin. Clearly, this was not someone who spent long days in an office cubicle.

THE JACKIE AND MARILYN REGIME

Both Jackie and Marilyn had their own personal regimes, tricks of the trade that helped them look so memorable.

Also, perhaps because they were of the same generation, they actually shared some beauty secrets (Erno Laszlo, Kenneth for hair).

Marilyn had massages and occasional colonics to lose weight quickly.

In the late 1950s and early 1960s, Jackie got B_{12} shots from Max Jacobson, a.k.a. Dr. Feelgood, which were basically amphetamines and vitamin B. He was the go-to guy for New York society and the New Frontier. "I don't care if it's horse piss, it works!" said JFK after Jacobson's ministrations helped his back pain. Anyone who was anyone went to him at one time or another—Marlene Dietrich, Truman Capote, photographer Mark Shaw, Leonard Bernstein. A socialite remembered that "you would run into *everyone* in the waiting room!"

MARILYN'S BEAUTY SECRETS

Like a true diva, MM was very reluctant to share her secrets, but we have unearthed a few. Writing to a fan, she said she had very few beauty tricks, but that she put her face in a sink filled with hot water—as hot as she could stand—morning and night.

As a devotee of the Erno Laszlo skin care system, she also rinsed her face thirty times after every wash.

When not wearing makeup, she might apply Vaseline, cold cream, lanolin, olive oil or hormone cream to her face as a protective agent.

Marilyn was famous for her seductive eyes. She once admitted that she lowered her eyelids a little just before the picture was snapped to make them look mysterious.

Marilyn wore false eyelashes and was one of the first women to meticulously cut them in half and apply them only to the outer edges of her eyelids.

Like JKO, she was a fan of Pond's Cold Cream. (Or we should say, because of the timing issue, that Jackie was following Marilyn's lead here—she used to slather it on her face and then sit outside on the porch and read manuscripts when she was on the Vineyard. Houseguests of her son John be damned!)

JACKIE'S BEAUTY SECRETS

Jackie never got stuck in a certain "look" and was always on the lookout for the latest beauty tips.

She used foundation by Elizabeth Arden.

Prior to a gala event hosted by the American Ballet Theatre in the 1980s, Jackie had her makeup done at her New York City apartment by a professional makeup artist a week before, to see how it would look. She wore a white dressing gown to match the color of the dress she intended to wear. Every time the makeup artist did something, Jackie took out her own hand mirror to see what she had done and then wrote it down, meticulously, on a yellow legal pad, so she could learn to do it in the future.

Left alone, her hair was somewhat kinky. To get that perfect "ladies who lunch" look, she had her hair blown out twice a week by Thomas Morrissey on the Upper East Side.

Like Marilyn, Jackie was also big on getting massages.

J+M: GETTING THE LOOK

We asked our favorite makeup guru, Darac, to give us some tips for getting the Jackie or Marilyn Look. Both women loved experimenting with makeup, so we say, "Go for it!"

JACKIE

According to Darac, the Jackie look is Classic Elegance—softly sculptured, approachable beauty and satin skin.

Brow

The brow should have a natural look with rounded arches; nothing in nature has a 45-degree angle. The brown should have a soft start, and then it should curve and end at the corner of the eye.

Eyes

Create soft and smoky eyes using neutral beige, taupe and dark brown eye shadow, soft pencil liner and thickening mascara.

Cheeks

Focus on the apples of the cheeks, and blend in cheek color with the rest of the face.

Use tapped-on and blended cream color.

Face

Dust the entire face with a soft veil of pink/peachy powder.

Lips

Apply lipstick or lip gloss first, then softly use liner to strengthen but not define the lip line.

MARILYN

Here, we are going for the Femme Fatale, definitely provocative! Aim for a more finished look and structured application, with eggshell skin.

Brow

Go for a severe arch that is full and defined. Definition is everything!

Eyes

Shadow should match skin tone to intensify the impact of the lash line.

Use lengthening mascara for intense lashes, with false lashes on the outer ends and liquid liner that curves up and away at the ends to match lashes.

Cheeks
Use very little color on the apples of the cheeks. Focus on defining the cheekbones.

Face
Porcelain-like; clean and even all over.

Lips
First line the lips, defining the top lip in a bow shape. Then apply lipstick, blot with tissue, apply powder over a tissue, and then reapply lipstick.

BOMBSHELL RED

Marilyn *owned* red lipstick. Owned it.

Red lipstick is a beauty trend that is currently, happily, back in style and emulated by everyone from Madonna and Gwen Stefani to Scarlett Johansson and Christina Hendricks. Back in the day, MM wore Shiseido in a color that is no longer available. But today's formulations are so much improved over those from the 1950s that you will barely notice.

Here is some advice to make red lipstick your own.

Skin tone. The most important thing in determining which red is right for you is your skin tone. Are you a warm red or a cool red?

If your skin has pink undertones, you should stick to reds that have a pink base. If you have warm yellow tones, look for a red with a golden or tawny base. If you are the classic pale and pink coloring, lipsticks with a touch of blue will be the best match.

Be prepared. When you are moisturizing your face, don't forget your lips, as you want them to be well cared for.

Conceal and protect. Using lip liner is essential with red lipstick. It helps to seal the color and prevents the ultimate red lipstick faux pas: bleeding. Liner also acts as great base for lipstick, so use it all over the lips. Try to use the same shade as the lipstick so it doesn't alter the finished look, or go with a shade that matches your natural lip color.

Brush strokes. When applying reds, always use a lip brush. It gives you much more control over where and how much color you are putting on. Apply lip color, blot with tissue, then reapply color and *don't* blot. This way, you'll get long-lasting color.

Some red lipsticks we like:

Lancôme, Chris and Tell (inspired by MM)

Jemma Kidd

Makeup School

Collection, Scarlett

Chanel Rouge Allure Laque, Dragon

SECRET SECRETS—THE JACKIE:
THINGS YOU MIGHT NOT KNOW ABOUT HER

Jackie could do ten push-ups at will, anytime, anywhere—real ones, not girl push-ups.

SECRET SECRETS—THE MARILYN:
THINGS YOU MIGHT NOT KNOW ABOUT HER

When she first began modeling, Marilyn had the widow's peak on her forehead removed with electrolysis.

4 | That Certain Something: Sex Appeal

"I'm only comfortable when I'm naked."

—MM

. . . .

"There are two kinds of women, those who want power in the world and those who want power in bed."

—JKO

For Jackie and Marilyn, *this* was the ball game—for they both understood a fundamental law of life: Sex is power.

Jackie and Marilyn reveled in being female and the advantages it gave them—because let's face it, the reality is that in dating or marriage, women have a great deal of leverage because they have the ability to say yes (or no).

And everyone knows that the right woman can vastly improve a man's life—or make it really, really bad.

Having said that, Jackie and Marilyn approached sex—and quite possibly viewed sex—in two fundamentally different ways.

Marilyn put it out there. If you saw Marilyn—in real life (please god), in a photograph, on the screen—it wasn't subtle. You knew what she was about and what she was offering you.

Jackie, on the other hand, was the exact opposite. She was sexy, but it was hidden. You might get there eventually (or you might not, ever), but she was going to make you work for it. And Jackie knew this about herself. Of her romantic life with JFK, she compared them to two icebergs and said, "The public life is above the water—the private life is submerged."

Marilyn's sexuality was present, obvious, very much in the forefront: She *was* sex.

Jackie revealed herself by withholding herself. Was it an upper-class thing? A 1950s thing? Maybe. (We think of Grace Kelly, a notorious sexpot in her youth.)

*M*arilyn fully embraced her sexuality and had no qualms or apologies about it. Once, famously, when asked what she wore in bed, she quipped, "Why, Chanel No. 5, of course." (Which was an amazingly risqué thing to say in 1955. The fact that it was true made it even more so.)

If Jackie was part of the Eastern establishment, that rapidly disappearing outpost of decorum, good manners and where you summer, Marilyn was all about escape. Release. "Who gives a damn?" Marilyn knew her appeal and worked it. "Men like happy girls," she noted and made a point of appearing light and carefree on a date no matter what was going on in her personal life. She might be privately heartbroken, she might be broke and half-starving, but boy, you were not going to hear about it.

While Jackie was far more publicly disciplined, with her enigmatic smile, whispery voice and ballet posture (who knew *what* she was thinking behind all that decidedly good form), there is the opposite sense that Marilyn would do anything, be anyone you wanted. This was especially powerful in the 1950s, when "good girls didn't," or at least not without the imprimatur of marriage.

And even then they might not.

Marilyn always gave the impression that she was up for anything—"Ever notice how 'What the hell' is always the right answer?" she once observed.

Jackie might be up for anything . . . eventually. But she was not known for giving it away. In college, the young men in her social set (using a term then popular) described Jackie as a "hold your meter, driver" type. They knew to have the taxi wait with the meter running when they walked her to the front door, because nothing was going to happen that night.

MARILYN COULD MELT YOU WITH HER EYES

Don't ever underestimate the power of sex and beauty. As photographer Lawrence Schiller observed, "Marilyn was very sensual. She knew how to handle her body. She knew how to handle her lips. With Marilyn, when everything was working, there was no one single element. She was in perfect harmony. She knew how to look into your eyes, and that was very, very powerful."

Combining a sense of humor with some measure of vulnerability—and Marilyn was far more publicly vulnerable than Jackie—she was almost irresistible to men.

> *"A sex symbol becomes a thing, and I just hate to be a thing. You're always running into people's unconscious. It's nice to be included in people's fantasies, but you also like to be accepted for your own sake. I don't look at myself as a commodity, but I'm sure a lot of people have. . . . If I'm sounding 'picked on,' I think I have been."*
>
> MARILYN ON BEING A SEX SYMBOL

JACKIE WAS THE BETTER KISSER. SHE WAS ALSO THE BETTER POKER PLAYER

While the Jackie Gal and the Marilyn Woman of today are both sensualists, the Jackie Gal is more guarded, less obvious in her sexual energy. Still, the sophisticated male knows it is there.

Surprisingly, the Jackie is the better kisser, if only because she grew up with a sister everyone considered prettier, while she was the smart one. Plus, she went to highly restrictive, all-girls' schools, so there were months, years even, to get very good at necking.

While Marilyn was very upfront and open in her dealings with the opposite sex, Jackie—having been caught in the cross-fire of her parents' divorce (when divorce was both stigmatized and a rarity) and tutored in the ways of men and women by her oh-so-cynical father—realized that it was, on one level, a game. And man, could she play it.

The Jackie MO in dealing with men is this: Accept the premise that a relationship is almost like a poker match (at least in its early stages). You have to be able to walk away, leaving your cards on the table at any time.

Another JKO corollary is that men get bored pretty easily, so you have to mix it up. For example:

1. Don't throw yourself at him.

2. Be very, very present.

3. Disappear for a while.

4. Oh, okay—throw yourself at him.

Pretend you're a major-league pitcher—mix up your game a bit. Call him first thing in the morning just to say hello, then accept a lot of dinner invites from other friends and ignore him for a week or so. Whatever you do, *don't* be an open book.

. . . .
How Was Jackie Sexy?
. . . .

Jackie was sexy in that you didn't expect it from her. In this way, she was almost the opposite of Marilyn—where Marilyn revealed (in a big way), Jackie withheld.

Like her romantic nemesis Grace Kelly, she appeared deeply conventional, but then she would say something to an aging dinner-partner (say, at a state dinner at the White House) and "his eyes would practically pop out of his head."

Aristotle Onassis (a man who certainly knew how to seduce a woman) called it when he said of Jackie, "She is a totally misunderstood woman. Perhaps she even misunderstands herself. She's being held up as a model of propriety, constancy and so many of those boring American female virtues. She's now utterly devoid of mystery. She needs a small scandal to bring her alive—a peccadillo, an indiscretion. Something should happen to her to win over fresh compassion. The world loves to pity fallen grandeur."

Less than a year later, they were wed.

. . . .

*H*ave No Problem with Nudity—Love your body, whatever its shape. When you get right down to it, most men are so thrilled to see a nude woman in any shape or form and at any time of the day or night that you don't need to be a perfect size 6 to be loveable. It's all about energy and how you view yourself, something our European counterparts have known for centuries.

It also helps to have a sense of humor about the whole thing. Once, asked what she had on during a nude calendar shoot she had posed for as a starving model/actress, the Real Marilyn quipped, "The radio."

"35-22-35"[1]

Whether you are planning to seduce someone or (god forbid) you get hit by a bus and end up in the emergency room, you want to look fabulous in your lingerie.

To get the expert's opinion on beautiful undergarments, we went to the source—Rebecca Apsan, owner of La Petite Coquette, the insider's lingerie shop favored by Cindy Crawford, Sarah Jessica Parker, Angelica Huston, Uma Thurman and sophisticated gals (and the men who love them) from all over.

To begin with, Apsan believes that 85 percent of women are wearing the wrong bra because "they're wearing the same size bra that their mother told them they should be wearing when they were fourteen years old!" Add that to the fact that there is no standardized sizing for brassieres, and it's no wonder most women's bras are not doing them any figure favors.

Instead, Apsan suggests that a woman go to her local lingerie shop and spend about forty-five minutes trying

[1] Marilyn's measurements.

on different sizes to see what fits her best. Apsan believes that an intimate wardrobe should contain four to six key pieces: everyday bras that are rotated, including basic T-shirt bras. You should also have two or three demi-cup or push-up bras in lace or a special color to "jumpstart your day" when you need it. Finally, you should have two strapless bras.

Bras should generally be nude or black, as white stands out too much.

More fun facts: Apsan confided to us that "the more sophisticated, classy women—the Jackies—are usually kinkier in bed. They'll push the envelope. The most proper looking girls are the ones wearing garter belts and stockings. The Marilyn types—the ones that are really obvious about putting it out there—want sex the least. . . ."

Finally, Apsan concludes, "A good bra is like a good man—good looking, supportive and never lets you down. . . ." Having experienced both, we agree.

THE SPANX SECRET

In case you are wondering how every woman between the ages of twenty and eighty has created a masterful MM/Joan Holloway silhouette for herself this season, we introduce you to Spanx®, the genius, genius undergarment that Sara Blakely invented.

If you don't know about these, you should.

Spanx fans range from Oprah to Gwyneth, from stylists to size-2 Upper East Side socialites. All swear by them to smooth out their figures. Beginning with a surprisingly comfortable body shaper, the line has been expanded to include camisoles, leggings to be worn under pants, and even brassieres. (We have heard, anecdotally, that some women wear two pairs at once for the ultimate in midsection control. But wow, even we can't imagine being this committed to looking a size smaller.)

In addition to inventing—on her own, on her living room floor—one of the most necessary contributions to modern feminine beauty since the lipstick (and we promise, we are not on the take here), Sara is also intensely cool and has started her own charitable organization to support and empower women around the world. She says, "I feel very blessed to have had my 'aha' moment in America, where women are free to start their own business."

Wow, *talk* about a Jackie/Marilyn Gal . . .

MARILYN KNEW HOW TO TURN IT ON (AND OFF)

Sex appeal was something that Marilyn, along with most women, could turn on or off. In fact, to her, "Marilyn Monroe" was almost a character that she created.

In New York City she once turned to a friend and said, "I can put on a polo coat and no makeup and get along pretty well. . . . Want to see me be her?"

And then she did.

Lawrence Schiller said that Marilyn "was really an actress. The 'dumb blonde' image was a total performance. She could turn it on and she could turn it off."

As he recalled, "I remember once I was walking with her from the parking lot to the dressing room. She had on this big black and white cardigan sweater. Her voice was very quiet and we were just talking about what she was going to do that afternoon. A couple of guys came around the corner, walking in the opposite direction towards her. And all of a sudden she became Marilyn Monroe, the dumb blonde. Her shoulders changed, her face changed. When they walked by, she turned her head over her shoulder and flashed that coquettish smile of hers— she was playing to them because she knew they wanted to see 'Marilyn Monroe.' "

THE MARILYN MIEN: ADORABLE DISHABILLE

In terms of style and manner—and dress—the Marilyn Gal is just a little bit looser than the Jackie Gal, on a lot of levels.

And even though her clothes are extremely fitted, there always seems to be a strap falling off her shoulder. (And if not actually slipping off her shoulder at this moment, there is always the impression of a strap *about* to fall off.)

Fully dressed (sitting in the midst of a major board meeting, for example), she seems as if she is about to fall out of her clothing, even if, in a nod to respectability (or the fall season), she is wearing a cashmere button-down cardigan.

Unlike the Jackie, the Marilyn is rarely still. The air around her is charged. Even sitting still (a thing to behold), she is always imperceptibly moving. This keeps everyone in her vicinity off balance.

Which is precisely the point.

Even her hair is sexy. While it might be "done," it was done for a date the night before, and here we are now, the following day. But even a bit dishabille, she still looks amazing.

She wears heels, naturally, 99.9 percent of the time and has an adorable habit of falling out of her slingbacks. Like a *Vogue* editor, the Marilyn rarely wears stockings, even in February. But if she does, they are Fogal up to the thigh (bought at Bloomingdale's or a little shop in the 7th Arrondissement she happened upon), sheer black, occasionally fishnet, never patterned or opaque—why waste the beautiful gams with too much window dressing, she figures. Should she go to the effort of the whole garter/merry widow routine, it is for a man she truly loves.

If the Marilyn is not in heels, she is barefoot at home or on a beach in Malibu, wearing bright red nail polish.

Alone or with company, she is the rare woman who can pull off marabou mules unironically.

And yet there is nothing untoward about our Marilyn—in some ways, she *was* America—the fun, sexy, childlike, trusting, noncynical part of America.

She was so open, so obvious, that there was nothing hidden about her desire, about what she might do for you. This is part of her charm, after all.

> *"Marilyn is a kind of ultimate. She is uniquely feminine. . . . She makes a man proud to be a man."*
>
> —CLARK GABLE

THE JACKIE MIEN: STRAITLACED. SORT OF.

The Jackie woman is "acceptable." We've established that. If you are up for an ambassadorship, partner at the law firm or have to close a business deal, you want her at your side.

Because of the breadth of her experience, Jackie can go high or low.

Speak French? She can do that better than you.

Get on a horse and ride (English or western)? Fine.

Head down to some juke joint in the Mississippi Delta (where they have never seen anyone like her before) and drink beer out of a bottle? No problem. She can do that *and* dance with the locals.

The great thing about the Jackie Gal is that she can roll with it. A Valentino gown or T-shirt and jeans, she can wear either with equal aplomb.

The true Jackie keeps her cards close to her chest. She can be ironic, quietly sarcastic among those she trusts. In this way, she is as great an actress as the Marilyn. After all, it was JKO who famously said, "Sex is a bad thing because it rumples the clothes." (She was *kidding*—we think.)

And what is she like in bed?

Memorable. Possibly because once you get her there and she trusts you, anything is possible.

Like most women, she equates sex with love. But she is no pushover. Like a true Leo, she is proud. She expects to be treated properly because she knows her worth. (If her father taught her nothing else, he taught her this.) She will not say a word, but ignore her or get her a crappy present for Christmas, and it will take some effort to regain her trust.

And by then, she is gone.

MARILYN'S POWER OVER MEN (AND SOME WOMEN)

While Jackie might be socially acceptable (for what that was worth in those days) or have gone to better schools (ditto), Marilyn held sway (sexual, emotional, obsessive, psychic) over men. Some people say this control over the opposite sex is what really matters, where all other success comes from.

"I don't mind being burdened with being glamorous and sexual," Marilyn said. "Beauty and femininity are ageless and can't be contrived, and glamour, although the manufacturers won't like this, cannot be manufactured. . . . We are all born sexual creatures, thank God, but it's a pity so many people despise and crush this natural gift. Art, real art, comes from it, everything."

Marilyn's power sprang from one essential fact. She could look into a man's eyes, smile (or not—it didn't matter), and get what she wanted. And she knew it. Her seductive powers, her *need* to be loved, worked with women, too. Her first drama coach, Natasha Lytess, devoted herself to Marilyn for years, proclaiming her love for her and almost becoming obsessed with her, as did another acting coach, Paula Strasberg, and (for some reason) her housekeeper, Eunice Murray.

Not knowing any better (one imagines her on the cusp of thirty or forty), she feared it could leave her with age, but it never did. Beauty is only part of Marilyn's sexual energy, that great Nile—but not all of it.

Unlike Jackie, Marilyn needed an audience—needed to be seen, to be recognized. She wanted to get the hell out of where she was from, not to be anonymous, to make her mark on the world. *Love me,* she seemed to say. Unlike Jackie, Marilyn needed her work. She needed to be known in a very public sphere (the only kind that matters, after all).

But still, it was never enough. And if the Marilyn Gal of today has not learned this yet, she will.

JACKIE'S POWER OVER MEN

How did Jackie do it? Well, she liked men, for starters. And this is a huge advantage. (You would be surprised at the number of women out in the world who don't.) She also knew that if a man had her by his side, she was an asset. She had that skill of the courtesan (that both of her husbands also had, actually): When she looked into your eyes and listened to you, there was no one else in the room. She listened. She heard. She remembered what you had said.

Like most professional wives, she was exceedingly thoughtful and really good on the follow-through, at perceiving what might make one's life easier (or just improved), without being told. When she visited London for Queen Elizabeth's coronation and had been dating JFK for a year with no sign of an engagement,[2] she lugged home a heavy suitcase full of rare hardcover books for him, paying $100 in extra charges—when $100 meant something—to get it on board.

Similarly, when she was married to Onassis, for some reason he loved Duncan Hines chocolate cake made from the box. Sure, he had a French chef on Skorpios, his private island, but he just really, really liked the way the Duncan Hines cake tasted. So Jackie made sure there were always several boxes on hand, flown in specially from New York.

It is this kind of attention to detail, the little things that matter, that made JKO a keeper.

On the other hand, Jackie did not have a ton of girlfriends. She went to all of those single-sex girls' schools through college, and frankly, large groups of women sort of drove her up the wall. She didn't know why, they just got on her nerves. Today's Jackie Gal has to be careful—she has such a strong personality that she tends to attract followers (the weaker willed are quickly turned into glorified secretaries or assistants). She knows she has this tendency. Which is why she prefers men.

BEING MARILYN: WHEN EVERYONE WANTS TO SLEEP WITH YOU

The Marilyn Gal of today has sex. A lot.

And when she isn't, she has lots of sexual energy—beaux,

. . . .

2 What can we say? The Kennedys, being Irish, liked long engagements. JFK's sister, Eunice, subjected poor Sarge to a seven-year courtship.

admirers, some guy she met two years ago on a plane coming back from the Vineyard over the Fourth of July weekend. He, of course, has been thinking about her since the morning they met. And wondering, *praying,* how he might run into her again. He even remembers her perfume, her hair, the dress she wore and exactly what she said to him. She doesn't remember him.

Some women get crushes on her, too. She pretends not to notice; she doesn't want to deal with it. It has happened before and will happen again. Eventually, it blows over.

As a side note, people tend to get obsessed with the Marilyn in a far more intense way than they do with the Jackie. It has always been like this.

Men do mad things to get her attention—write poetry (even if they can't write),[3] invite her to London to go to a matinee, give her a puppy as a gift.[4]

The Marilyn knows that she is the person they are all so attracted to, of course. But sometimes she almost feels as if all the attention has nothing to do with her. Like "Marilyn" is a construct she has created that she can turn off or on at will.

When she is in a funny mood she thinks, of course everyone wants to sleep with her—they can't help it! Heck, *she* sleeps with her and almost can't believe her good fortune.

She's kidding.

(Sort of.)

She has found herself in these situations since she was fifteen years old, and as a result, the Marilyn likes being around women and gay men because she can relax and let her guard down. She also loves children and animals; she loves their innocence and the fact that they don't want anything from her. For this reason, she is a big supporter of the ASPCA. She cannot

. . . .

3 In another life, the Marilyn would have hung with Carl Sandburg. Today, it is just as likely to be Russell Simmons and his Def Jam poetry.

4 And for the M, it really is the thought that counts . . . forget diamonds—give her a puppy or a hardcover book she has not read yet, and see how she reacts.

bear to even walk by a pet store with puppies in the window; she wants to adopt them all.

Crowds of men frighten her the most.

AND WHICH ARE YOU?

In assessing your own situation—in determining whether you are a Jackie or a Marilyn—it is important to realize that although the Marilyn appears outwardly more sexual, the Jackie does not enjoy sex any less. She is simply less obvious about it.

What we are saying is this: Look beyond the first, obvious appearances. The Marilyn of today can go to Harvard; the deeply aspirational Jackie might work at Starbucks.

J+M—THE BARE ESSENTIALS

Although sex appeal is (of course) indefinable, for Jackie and Marilyn, it can be broken down into a few essentials.

. . . .

THE VOICE

. . . .

In real life (no matter how they presented themselves in public and on screen), both Jackie and Marilyn spoke in low, dulcet tones. Friends who knew Jackie said that her "real" voice was low and even a bit masculine; in fact, meeting her for the first time over a late-night dinner at P. J. Clarke's, one female friend said she was surprised at how direct and outspoken Jackie was. The fey, whispery voice was something she put on when she was anxious about speaking in public. (If you really want to hear what she sounded like, listen to JKO speak in a foreign language—either French or Spanish.)

Similarly, Marilyn's "movie voice" was a bit of a fake. Lawrence Schiller observed that MM's voice was "an octave or two lower" than what you would expect. The movie Marilyn voice was almost an extreme example of seduction: breathy, languid, with a hint of uncertainty behind it. Even when ordering a cup of coffee, she seemed to be whispering promises in your ear.

. . . .

THE WALK
. . . .

While their voices were similar, Jackie and Marilyn each had very distinctive walks. While JKO glided as subtly as a geisha through official state functions in the White House, revealing little,[5] and her private years away from Washington were characterized by a very fast, athletic gait, Marilyn (often hours late) made an entrance when she walked into a room and always made a point of wearing clothing that emphasized her assets.

Jackie withheld while Marilyn revealed.

. . . .

WORDS HAVE POWER
. . . .

Jackie, perhaps taking a page from Marilyn's *Some Like It Hot* playbook, would say the most outlandish thing to world leaders, who were mostly old men and used to being catered to. And it worked. Upon being introduced to JFK during the very stressful Vienna summit, Nikita Khrushchev said, "I want to shake *her* hand first."

Later, speaking with Khrushchev during a formal dinner, Jackie said, "Oh Mr. Premier—don't bore me with your silly statistics. . . ."

As Jackie knew, you can say some pretty outrageous things if there is a smile in your voice (which is why email can get you in so much trouble; it doesn't convey the tone of what you are saying).

. . . .

5 The White House press office was instructed by JKO: "I want minimum information given with maximum politeness."

SECRET SECRETS—THE MARILYN: THINGS YOU MIGHT NOT KNOW ABOUT HER

Marilyn knew that the way a man can really get to a woman is through her brain: "If you can make a girl laugh, you can make her do anything."

SECRET SECRETS—THE JACKIE: THINGS YOU MIGHT NOT KNOW ABOUT HER

From all reports, JFK was not a very attentive lover. Ari was.

5 : Dating and Courtship

"No serious interests, but I'm always interested. . . ."

—MM, WHEN ASKED IF SHE WAS DATING OR IN LOVE

. . . .

"Jackie had more men per square inch than any woman I have ever known."

—LETITIA BALDRIGE

Jackie and Marilyn both instinctively played to men, but in a different way. "Marilyn's supposed helplessness was her greatest strength," said Arthur Miller, while Jackie also worked the "little girl lost" thing (although not to the degree Marilyn did).

JKO's father adored her and instilled in her the knowledge that she was special (among other things, he counseled her on dating, telling her that "all men are rats"), while MM's father was absent, and her difficult childhood set her up for a lifetime where it was impossible for her *not* to play up to a man. (She turned men on with this act and enjoyed the power of it).[1]

. . . .

1 Intriguingly, MM had a childhood fantasy that Clark Gable was her father, while JKO's actual father really did look like Clark Gable. In 1960, MM filmed *The Misfits* with Gable.

Both were attracted to powerful men and had powerful older protectors—Marilyn was discovered by Hollywood superagent Johnny Hyde, while Jackie had the patriarch Joseph P. Kennedy in her corner. Marilyn Monroe was married three times—to James Dougherty, Joe DiMaggio and Arthur Miller. Jacqueline Onassis was married twice, to John F. Kennedy and Aristotle Onassis, a man twenty-three years her senior. (It is said that she "stole" him from her sister, Lee Radziwill, who was originally dating him before he turned his attention to Jackie. In an infamous anecdote, Janet Auchincloss once stormed into Onassis's suite at Claridge's Hotel in London, looking for her daughter. Dressed in a bathrobe and smoking a cigar, Onassis drawled, "And who is your daughter?" "The Princess Radziwill!" Mrs. Auchincloss huffed. "In that case, Madame," Onassis said, "she just left.")

After Onassis's death, Jackie had a longstanding relationship with diamond merchant Maurice Tempelsman.

*W*ith the Jackie and Marilyn Gals of today, relating to men is perhaps a matter of degree and circumstance. There are times in life when it is more advantageous to be more Jackie (when meeting your possible future mother-in-law, for example), and other times when it is better to be a full-on Marilyn (say, the proverbial third date).

But in any event, neither Jackie nor Marilyn ever fell into the demeaning *He's Just Not That Into You* single-gal construct that has been created today. Whether dating, dealing with a director, married, or meeting Nikita Khrushchev, Marilyn and Jackie always had the upper hand with the opposite sex.

In earlier chapters, we explored two pillars of the essential Jackie or Marilyn appeal—sex and beauty. (The third, in case you're wondering, is intelligence.) But between sex and beauty, well, there is the really fun stuff of men, dating and courtship.

THE JACKIE AND THE MARILYN REAL-WORLD DATING TIPS

(Sort of like *The Rules,* but hipper and more life-enhancing.)

*B*etween the two of them, Jackie and Marilyn knew pretty much everyone worth knowing in the latter part of the 20th century. Name a man of talent or stature on either the East or West Coast (or Paris, London, Skorpios and Dublin, for that matter), and Jackie or Marilyn had met, dated, knew, worked with, admired, flirted with, befriended, bedded or possibly been engaged and/or married to him.

Winston Churchill? Check. Bill Holden? Check. Hubert de Givenchy, Walter Winchell, Darryl Zanuck, Marlon Brando, the maitre d' of the Stork Club, the Kennedy boys? Joe DiMaggio? Truman Capote? (And in Jackie's case, since she lived longer, Valentino, Bill Clinton, Mikhail Baryshnikov, Mick Jagger and Deepak Chopra? Check, check and check.)

And what does this mean for you, oh J+M Gal? Well for starters, get out there and meet people! It doesn't matter how you do it—travel, volunteer, take a friend who is having a bad day out to lunch, just get out of the house—you never know what might happen out there.

> **Flirt Like Hell**—Both the Jackie and the Marilyn Gal flirt like hell with pretty much everything that moves—men, women, puppies, babies, senior citizens, the downstairs neighbor. They can't help it; it's just the way they are.
>
> The world is a stage, and once the Marilyn walks out her front door, she is *on.* And it should be the same for you. Every day is an audition. Every waking moment is full of verdant, romantic possibilities. The way the Marilyn sees it, if she walks past a construction site and no one notices her, she's doing something wrong. If she walks out her front door and the doorman doesn't instinctively smile at her—*what?*

She knows that men are visual creatures, and for whatever reason, they like to look at her. In the Marilyn's view, that's okay, because life is hard enough, and if someone can make you laugh or lift your spirits (or vice versa), that's always a good thing.

In our grandmothers' day, they called it charm. Take our word for it: It still works. But keep it light—gather some pointers from how well MM flirted with grumpy Larry Olivier in *The Prince and the Showgirl*.

Jackie, on the other hand, goofs around with men, keeps them on their toes, kind of makes fun of them, almost in spite of their worldly success and power. In 1957, she and Senator Kennedy were invited on Aristotle Onassis's yacht to meet Winston Churchill, one of JFK's idols. The former prime minister was quite elderly and seemed to ignore JFK or not quite know who he was. After they left, Kennedy was bereft at having failed to connect with his idol.

"Maybe he thought you were a waiter," said Jackie mischievously, taking note of his white dinner jacket.[2]

Keep a Lot of Men Hanging Around—Seventy-year-old confirmed bachelors, couturier designers, former beaux still pining away, the seventeen-year-old delivery boy from the butcher shop downstairs—who cares? Whether you are married, dating or single,[3] what you want is masculine energy. That way, you are happy and it keeps everyone (yourself included) from getting complacent. Some happy hunting grounds include major league baseball games, the Dartmouth Winter Carnival and the gym.

One of our best friends met the man she married (yes, married) on a subway. And he's terrific. Another

. . . .

2 Another anecdote: JKO's private nickname for Onassis (after their marriage) was "Goldfinger" after the extremely rich Bond baddie.
3 And, some would say, especially if you are married.

(we kid you not) met the handsomest man in New York in an elevator. They worked on completely different floors, but he tracked her down on Valentine's Day by sending one of his officemates to her door with a hand-made card.

Or heck, if you are a Marilyn, just going down to the local Starbucks any given morning can work just fine.

And forget expensive moisturizers and dubious plastic surgery—what is it the French say? *"Elle doit être amoureuse, elle a arrêté de porter la fondation."*[4] If nothing else, both the Jackie and the Marilyn know that having a lot of admirers keeps them looking young and everyone on their toes.

Mum's the Word—And yet, be wildly discreet about the specifics of who you are actually dating. No matter what the papers intimated, Marilyn always referred to Joe DiMaggio and Arthur Miller (husbands number two and three) as "Mr. DiMaggio" and "Mr. Miller." Jackie was engaged to John Husted the entire time she was being courted by JFK. "Don't believe all that stuff you hear about Jack Kennedy," she assured Husted.

When it comes to your personal life, a bit of mystery never hurt anyone, and besides, the person you are really involved with knows who he is—and that's all that matters, right?

Absence Really Does Make the Heart Grow Fonder— If you're not getting the attention you feel you deserve in the romance department, split. Take a break. Hit the road and ignore his emails. Tell him your iPhone ran out of batteries or something. Better yet, leave the country.

· · · · · · · · · · · · ·
4 "She must be in love, she's stopped wearing foundation."

A BRIEF TIME-OUT—MM HAD HER OWN
DATING RULES: NONE

Okay, as J+M Gals, we have shared some rules, but here's the thing we have to admit—Marilyn was so desired by *everyone* that she had no rules. She did whatever the hell she wanted at all times.

Even she admitted it—"When I was 11, the whole world suddenly opened up. Every fellow honked his horn. The world

became friendly. . . ." She walked out her door and had men literally following her down the street. (Which, now that we think of it, actually sounds kind of scary in real life.)

After ending her first marriage to James Dougherty and moving to Hollywood, she began to have some small success in minor roles and got even more attention from powerful studio heads Jack Warner and Joseph Schenck, producer Darryl Zanuck and others.

But even then, among the hotshot agents and studio presidents who could further her career, MM was an equal-opportunity dater. A reporter from *LIFE*, doing an early piece on her, tells of being with her at the Chateau Marmont and some poor guy showing up at her door with a dozen roses— a day early for their date . . . or maybe Marilyn got the date mixed up and thought it was the next night. But at any rate, the poor shlub left the roses and went sadly on his way.

But you know what? It didn't matter—do you think he was back the next night with a new bouquet hoping she would be there? Absolutely.

Because let's face it: If you are pretty enough to whomever you are dating, every rule gets tossed out the window.

THE J+M LIFE LESSON—BELIEVE WHAT HE TELLS YOU

A man will always tell you who he is, where he is in the world and what he has on his mind (especially in regard to you). The smart Marilyn or Jackie listens. In real life, it never took Jackie long (say, about thirty-five seconds) to get the lay of the land in any situation, particularly when it came to possible romantic partners. And then she did what was best for her.

After she graduated from college, she began dating a very nice guy, John Husted.[5] His family was in the *Social Register*. He was a friend of her father, Jack Bouvier, and the Auchin-

. . . .
5 And, ladies, with the description "very nice guy," you know where this is going. . . .

closses. He was a stockbroker. He went to Yale and summered in Nantucket. In short: He was very acceptable.

After a few months, he and Jackie got engaged, as was the custom in 1951. Shortly thereafter, there was an announcement in the *New York Times*.

In May 1951, prior to the engagement, Jackie met then–Senator John F. Kennedy at a Georgetown dinner party hosted by their friends Charles and Martha Bartlett—who had been trying for months to get the two of them together. There was a brief overlap between Husted and JFK, with Jackie (admitting nothing to either man) eventually returning the engagement ring and her mother placing a small "calling off the engagement" notice in the newspapers.

At the time, Jackie admitted to friends that Husted was too "immature" and "sedate" for her taste (well, he was a stockbroker). In later years, Husted felt that Jackie's mother got between them, intimating that he did not earn enough money to support Jackie—although in the 1950s, $17,000 a year was an extremely good salary.[6]

Marilyn, for her part, never looked at her dating life so strategically—or, well, strategically at all. While she went to poker nights at Joe Schenck's home (he was the powerful studio head of 20th Century Fox) on Sunday night and laughed and joked and emptied ashtrays with the best of the up-and-coming starlets, she was just as comfortable—probably more so—getting chili at Howard Johnson's in Times Square with a fellow student from the Actors Studio.

Marilyn's opinion of relations between the sexes was much less prosaic than Jackie's. More than anything, she believed in love, and she would not sell out for it. "It's often just enough to be with someone. I don't need to touch them. Not even talk. A feeling passes between you both. You're not alone."

. . . .

6 Ever the gentleman, Husted never spoke to the press about his time spent with Miss Bouvier.

Marilyn Monroe: (Literal) Heartbreaker

Johnny Hyde was a powerful older agent (fifty-three years old to Marilyn's twenty-three) who is credited with discovering Marilyn Monroe. Best friends with all of the studio bosses in Hollywood, he was a man who could—and did—do a lot for Marilyn in the early years of her career. He paid for her slight rhinoplasty and encouraged her to go platinum blonde. He also got her a screen test and hired at 20th Century Fox after they had turned her down two years earlier.

Hyde was not only powerful and respected, he was also madly in love with Marilyn and begged her to marry him repeatedly. But she knew that she was not in love with him and turned him down.

Hyde begged her.

He even moved out of his home and left his wife and three children to show Marilyn how serious he was about being with her. He was sick, with a heart condition, and was convinced that he would not live long. He assured Marilyn that as his widow, he would leave her a wealthy woman, respected in the small company town. Marilyn refused. She loved him as a friend, sure. But not in that way.

Shortly thereafter, Joe Hyde died of a heart attack, and his family closed ranks, refusing to allow Marilyn to attend the funeral. She was devastated.

You Don't Change Anyone!

In Date World (as in friendships), choose who you spend your time with wisely. A man is not a car—you can't remake him or turn him into your personal project. Oh, sure, you can change minor things like getting him a better haircut or eyeglasses, or a preference for cashmere or suede loafers, but you can't teach him thoughtfulness, grace, kindness, style or a sense of humor.

If You're Not Happy, Dump His Sorry A**—Tough but

true. Not to get too Oprah here, but love is supposed to make you feel happy. It is supposed to be positive. We are not saying there won't be a few bumps along the road, but not while you are dating! The entire dating/courtship phase is supposed to be fun.

While a perfect set of washboard abs is nice,[7] look at his character. Keep an eye out for gambling problems, addiction, abusive behavior—see how he treats the waitstaff. Does he raise his voice to you? Is he dismissive of your opinion when you try to broach sensitive subjects? If he is divorced, how does he treat his children? His former wife? Does he fulfill his commitments or expect them to live on $17 a month?[8]

THE SEVEN-YEAR ITCH. IN REAL LIFE.

"Husbands are chiefly good as lovers when they are betraying their wives."—MM

To hit the historical reset button here, both Jackie and Marilyn were involved with married men at various times in their lives. (If it matters, Jackie more publicly than Marilyn, although never while she was married.)

For Jackie, maybe it had something to do with her history, as both her father and her husbands were noted philanderers. After JFK's assassination, the men Jackie publicly dated were described as "very married, very old, or very queer." Not seeming to mind that many of her escorts were married, she went out with Mike Nichols, Peter Duchin, Gianni Agnelli and Frank Sinatra, among others. Her relationship with Ros Gilpatric, who served as Kennedy's deputy secretary of defense, became publicly known after a romantic letter

7 Extremely.
8 And then bitch about it to you. Charming.

she wrote him while on her honeymoon with Aristotle Onassis (explaining her recent, as-secret-as-possible marriage to Ari) was stolen and leaked to the press, causing Gilpatric's third wife, Madelin, to file for divorce shortly thereafter.

And Marilyn? Well, she *was* Marilyn Monroe, possibly the most desired female in the entire world—then and now—and had everyone from T. S. Eliot to Orson Welles to Yves Montand (her costar in *Let's Make Love*) to Arthur Miller (whom she eventually married and later divorced) to JFK and RFK after her.[9]

And how is this applicable today? As true Jackie/Marilyn Gals, we have very few rules when it comes to affairs of the heart—want to send him flowers? Go right ahead. (We have one friend who sent a bouquet to her beau on a construction site. Now *that* made a statement among all the guys, who then wanted to meet her.) Sex on the first date? Sex on the seventieth date?

We don't care. We really don't.

But when it comes to dating, we have one no-kidding-around rule: Don't get involved with a married man. (And if you are a guy, the same goes for a married woman.)

Maybe it's deeply confident, maybe it's wildly egotistical (okay, we cop to both), but whether you are seriously dating someone or just palling around, you are top dog. No scraps, no second place.

Besides, with all of your life experience and inherent Jackie/Marilyn fabulousness, you know there are a lot of fish in the sea. All you have to do is walk out the door to meet people. Lots and lots and lots of terrific, handsome, wonderful men who are insane about your fabulous self. And if he is that enamored with you, he can take care of business and get a proper divorce before you get involved in his life.

. . . .

9 As well as Marlon Brando, Frank Sinatra, Richard Burton and Elia Kazan.

If all the married people want to run around like they're in a badly cast Updike novel, that's their deal. You're not the one breaking up a family.

(And if nothing else, think of the heavy, heavy karma on that last decision.)

THE JKO DATING MO

When she first began dating, Jackie seemed to want to present herself as *less than*. Was it something girls were taught in the 1950s, so as not to intimidate possible beaux? Was it in the water? According to *Time* magazine, Jackie almost seemed to fear scaring her friends away by being both beautiful and bright and often hid her intelligence behind a mask of school-girl innocence.

Recalled her friend, socialite Jonathan Isham, "She was so much smarter than most of the people around her that she sublimated it. . . . She sometimes came across as a wide eyed, sappy type. It's pure defense. When I'd take her to the Yale Bowl, and it'd be fourth down and five to go, she'd say to me, 'Oh, why are they kicking the ball?' I'd say, 'Come on, Jackie, none of that.' She felt she ought to play up to the big Yaleman. The truth is, she probably knew more about football than I did."

And yet JFK (no slouch in the brain department himself) recognized Jackie's intellectual gifts early on and was attracted to her for them. She never acted like a lightweight for him.

A friend of JFK's said that Jackie was unlike any of his other girlfriends, who tended toward the "Dallas cheerleader, glamour girl type. . . . Jackie had substance." His secretary, Anne Lincoln, noticed that JFK always called Jackie himself to ask her out, instead of relegating the duty to her.

J+M FIELD NOTES: DATING DEAL BREAKERS

The Big Three:

1. Drug/alcohol abuse

2. Demeaning behavior

    This includes putting you down in public, cheating, being dismissive toward you, checking out other women in front of you, or any kind of weird sexual stuff you are uncomfortable with.

3. Dishonesty

    Lying, not keeping his word. Because frankly, life's too damn short to put up with such nonsense. It's one thing if a guy is shy or takes too long to get to the punch line of a joke. It's another thing if he is less than truthful . . . or makes promises that he has no intention of keeping.

There are also the satellite transgressions—

Forgetting Your Birthday. As a Leo, Jackie loved her birthday. She thought of it as "Christmas in July." Frankly, we can't imagine anyone forgetting our birthday—or yours—but if he does . . . out.

Being Mean to Your Dog—This is not even worth discussing. On par with (well, worse than) forgetting your birthday. Even the slightest transgression in this category and you are O.U.T. out!—ciao, lose my number, darling.

Not Tipping; Dissing the Help—We shouldn't even have to spell this one out for you, oh intrinsically fabulous one. Even when she was a struggling model/actress, the real Marilyn always tipped. If he doesn't, you should. And let that be the last you see of him.

General Jerkiness—There are several character traits we don't like in a man or woman—prejudice, small-mindedness, pessimism, grumpiness, complainers, warmongering, any kind of drama, watching FOX television (Kidding! Kidding!).

It is all about energy. Any relationship you have, whether it is with your mom, the butcher, your trainer, the accountant, your agent, the hairdresser, should be uplifting and positive. If not, it's time to do some rethinking and consider culling the inbox. (More difficult to do with your parents and close family members, granted.)

And not to get too metaphysical (oh, what the heck, the rest of the world is), but you can't meet the one you are *supposed* to be with if Mr. Negative is taking up so much of your space and time. But the real question, whether you are a Jackie or a Marilyn, is this: Why would you want to share your terrific life with a guy like this, anyway?[10]

And do you really think you are going to maintain your essential Jackie/Marilyn gorgeousness surrounded by such negative energy?

Exactly.

JKO CONVERSATIONAL GAMBITS

Jackie said very little about herself on a date. She knew that men love to talk about themselves, and if a woman encourages this, she quickly gains a reputation for being a great conversationalist.

There were two secrets to the JKO conversational arsenal that apply even today. The first is focus, focus, focus, and allow the person speaking to you to feel as if he is the only person in the entire world. (Supreme seducers like JFK, Pamela Harriman, Peter Duchin and Bill Clinton used this to great effect.)

. . . .

10 No one is that good in bed.

Second, Jackie paid attention to everything someone said and used even the simplest conversation to gain insight into a person. So if you say *one thing,* the Jackie Gal of today is going to remember it forever and bring it up—if she has to—at an opportune time. She wouldn't throw it in your face during an argument (she is both too kind and too smart for that) or bring it up after you've had a hard day at work (she knows the brutal Darwinism of the office), but in some ways, the Jackie is like a four-year-old . . . you say one thing, make one promise, one offhand remark, and she is going to remember it forever.[11]

QUICKTESTS

The Marilyn Quicktest: The man says "I love you" first. Always.

The Jackie Quicktest: You think that what goes on between a man and a woman is the most fascinating game of all. And you are very good at it.

---

11 And with her almost scary recall, she will probably be able to tell you what you were wearing, where the conversation took place, what she was wearing . . . (you get the idea).

J+M FIELD NOTES: HOW TO WRITE A LOVE LETTER

Hard as it is for the younger set to believe, in Jackie and Marilyn's day, there were three options for getting a hold of someone to let them know what was going on in your life. First, **the telephone,** which was expensive for anything other than local calls. Plus, there was generally one phone per household, and you did not pick up the phone every three minutes and call someone to discuss something trivial, like *American Idol.* A long-distance call usually meant bad news; i.e., someone had died or gotten drafted into the Korean War. **Second, the telegram** (again, bad news). These were transmitted to the local Western Union office, and a messenger showed up via bicycle on your doorstep to deliver it. Or, third, you sent **a letter or postcard.**

So, slightly off topic, but if you were going to meet someone, you had to make plans well in advance, make them very specific and *not change them.* If you were late, if the train was delayed, if you spaced and "forgot" you were supposed to meet your friend, he or she could wait hours for you to arrive. Or you might miss one another by showing up at the wrong spot, or he or she might be waiting for you (in the old days, people seemed to have less trouble simply waiting) and meet someone else and fall in love with *that* person—hence setting up the plot of practically every single 1940s heartbreak movie.

While it might surprise no one that Jackie was an inveterate letter writer, so was Marilyn. But first, the stationery. Both Jackie and Marilyn wrote their letters on really great stationery—Marilyn's (befitting her station as a world-famous actress) was simply embossed with her name on the top and on the back of the envelope, while Jackie's bore the address of her residence (3307 N Street; 1095 North Ocean Boulevard, Palm Beach, Florida; The White House).

Both wrote their letters by hand. Marilyn had the invented, dramatic penmanship of someone who had grown used to signing autographs, while Jackie bore the well-bred backward slant of a Farmington girl—the sort of handwriting seen in Diana Vreeland, Babe Paley and Princess Diana.

Both letter writers were inventive and showed insightful—if humorous—analysis of events of the day. Face it: If you got a letter from either Jackie or Marilyn, you were going to keep it. (And most did.)

Now, on to your own *billets doux*. How to write a love letter à la Jackie or Marilyn?

Okay, right off the bat, with all of the forgettable cell phone, email, Twitter and IM nonsense going back and forth, if you take the time to write anything longer than two sentences, put it in an envelope and send it via U.S. mail, you are way ahead of the pack. In the old days (forget your parents' generation—say, five years ago) people still wrote letters. Now, only those with an eye toward posterity do.

Type it so that he can read what you are saying. Be like Marilyn and scrawl your name at the bottom with great abandon, as if you are a Hollywood star. Give the impression that this is no big deal: You send dozens of these notes to your admirers. (Which you probably do.)

Regarding content, in some ways, it almost does not matter what the note says. It can be four sentences; it can be two and a half typed pages (single spaced) of whatever is on your mind. You can discuss Descartes. You can discuss a great pair of shoes you saw in a shop window. If you are entertaining enough, it does not matter.

Whatever you do, do not mention the word "love" in the letter. Do not tell him how great he is (that is for him to tell you), do not tell him you miss him, do not thank him for being in your life, do not ask him where the "relationship is going" (zzzzzzzzzzzzzzzzzzzzzz).

If you are feeling warmhearted, thank him for his friendship. This will keep him off balance. (Friendship? He will read it and think to himself, and then start to get very, very worried.)

Other topics include: You are packing to leave for Paris but wanted to get this in the mail; you are en route to Paris; you are in Paris *at this very moment*; the Red Sox made the playoffs.

Similarly, do not sign "love" unless you are engaged. In that case, all bets are off, and you can do whatever you want.

Be sure to write "PERSONAL" on the back flap so that his secretary/assistant does not open it by mistake. Marilyn spritzed her letters with perfume, but personally (unless he is serving in the armed forces overseas), we think this is a bit much.

Send it to the office. Men find the combination of business-like (his typed address on the front) and personal (your note inside) particularly compelling.

And let's face it: Most guys working in offices are bored out of their minds and just looking for something to break up the monotony of the day. If he gets an actual letter in the mail and realizes it's from you, forget it—he can close the door, ask his assistant to hold his calls, open it carefully with a letter opener (remember those?), put his feet up on the desk and take his time reading it.

Once he has read it a few times (with his feet still up on the desk), he will fold it back up carefully, look out the window at the sky for a while and think of what a lucky S.O.B. he is to have you in his life. He might then take the letter from his desk again, carefully reread it, and have a very Cary Grant moment.

Anything you can do to make a man feel like Cary Grant in this day and age is not to be underestimated.

. . . .

AN APOCRYPHAL PICKUP LINE
. . . .

We have no idea if this is true, but what a great story.

Albert Einstein and Marilyn sat next to each other at a dinner party. After a few flutes of champagne, she cooed in his attentive ear, "I want to have your child. With my looks and your brains, it will be a perfect child!"

Einstein replied, "But what if it has my looks and your brains?"

We don't think this story is true because 1) there is no evidence that AE and MM ever met, and 2) the same story is often told of George Bernard Shaw and Isadora Duncan. But still— what if they *had*?

J+M FIELD NOTES: WHO PAYS FOR DINS?

On a date, the Marilyn could (maybe hypothetically *perhaps*) pay for dinner, especially when seated across from a starving but exceptionally cute artist.[12] After all, she knows what it is to be hungry.

The Jackie? Never.

Never. Never. Never. Never. Never. Never.

To say that it might even enter her mind to pay for a man in a date situation is beyond the realm of comprehension— like walking off the roof and flying. It is a matter of personal respect, after all.

Plus, the guy has the distinct privilege of sitting across a table from her while she focuses her attention on him (and is seen in public doing so). Having said this, the Jackie Woman of today is careful not to order anything too expensive if she thinks it might be an issue with her man. As long as he is understandably half in love with her, she is just as happy sitting with him on a park bench and eating an ice cream cone as she is having dinner at Daniel.

J+M FIELD NOTES: HOW TO SEND A MAN FLOWERS

Sending a man flowers is sort of like kissing him (bear with us). In the same way that you kiss the way you want to be kissed, only send flowers that you would like to receive. Both the Jackie and the Marilyn have been the recipient of so many bouquets that they could practically open their own flower shop with their expertise. (And on Valentine's Day—

. . . .
12 And we mean really cute—like (generationally speaking) Robert Pattinson or James Dean cute.

forget it!—the Marilyn gets so many arrangements that her home begins to resemble a hospital room or a mobbed-up funeral parlor, albeit with good design sense. She compensates by anonymously leaving them on the doorsteps of several of her neighbors the next morning and never admitting where they came from.[13])

In the same way that you would send what you would like to receive, we are also of the personal opinion that you only send flowers to a guy you know really well (i.e., your boyfriend, brother or husband). And even then, sparingly, say, once a year (if that).

Of course, the man can send you flowers as often as he wants—once a month, once a week. When he is in the doghouse. We have one friend who was being courted by someone she didn't really want to go out with. He sent progressively larger and larger bouquets to her place of work every day for almost a month. It got so bad that the receptionist and her coworkers were taking bets on what the next day's floral cavalcade might bring.

Wanting to bring an end to the petal-tastic onslaught, she finally agreed to go out with him.

They were married in less than a year.

*O*kay, back to basics. In general, we like compact arrangements. They are less fussy. You don't want to get too dramatic with the floral arrangement (no excessive height, no stalky things that no one knows where they came from and please—no baby's breath). In short, nothing that might embarrass the guy.

We also like a tight grouping of the same flower, and generally the same color—roses, tulips, daffodils in the spring, daisies, even. Again, you want to make a statement, but you also want it to look natural, unobtrusive and sort of cool, like you know what you are doing. In terms of color, about the only thing we

. . . .

13 Oh, they can probably figure it out.

would not do is send a man a dozen red long-stem roses. We don't even like them for ourselves—too Miss America—and they have far too many romantic 1950s-ish overtones to ever send to a man.

When you call the florist, let them know what you have in mind and where it is going. If they ask, describe the recipient to them. See what is in season or in the market that day, but make sure you express what you envisioned. For example, if we were sending a bouquet to a man, we would see what they had in shades of blue—light blue, purple (maybe), lilac even, with some smaller white flowers for accents. Freesia always smells terrific. Never yellow, pink or (with rare exceptions) white.

If you don't feel like having a florist send them, another option would be to gather a bunch of flowers from your garden and make a bouquet of your own, again keeping them low and tight and tying a wide ribbon around the neck of the vase to give it a little personality.

And the note? Nothing too mushy. The flowers are enough of a statement.

At the end of the day we want to make one thing clear, whether you are sending or receiving flowers—it truly does not matter what you send; it is the thought that counts. And the fact that you were thoughtful enough to send a bouquet of flowers is what he will remember.

Really.

A REALLY GREAT MM DATE STORY

While Jackie was the queen of America, Marilyn could have been Princess of Monaco. In the early 1950s, Aristotle Onassis cooked up the idea of polishing the fading fortunes of Monaco (described by Somerset Maugham as "a sunny place full of shady people") by having Prince Rainier marry an American film star. Onassis thought Marilyn Monroe would be perfect for the role (as it were) and suggested the idea to her representatives.

At first, Marilyn thought the whole thing was a goof ("Prince

Reindeer," she dubbed Rainier, giggling, to her girlfriends) and wasn't even sure where Monaco was. In Africa, perhaps?

For his part, Onassis wondered whether Rainier would want to marry Monroe.

Marilyn—no slouch when it came to gauging her own desirability—said, "Give me two days alone with him, and of course he'll want to marry me."

Eventually cooler heads prevailed, and Rainier was introduced to Grace Kelly, and the rest, as they say, is history.

Grace, interestingly, had her own connection to Jackie and the Kennedys. Growing up in Philadelphia, the daughter of a self-made bricklayer millionaire, the Irish Catholic Kellys were—if possible—even more photogenic and athletic than the Kennedys. Of course, the families knew one another, and JFK and Grace dated. After JFK and Jackie were married, Jack had to endure a brutal back operation at the Hospital for Special Surgery in New York. To cheer him up, Jackie (who had run into Grace at a dinner party) had Grace dress up as a nurse and surprise him.

Jack was so groggy and in pain that he didn't seem to recognize her. About twenty minutes later, Grace left his hospital room, despondent. "I must be losing my touch," she said.

After Grace married Rainier, Marilyn sent her a congratulatory telegram: "So glad you've found a way out of this business."

JFK, perhaps not the most thoughtful husband in the world, said to Jackie as they watched the newsreel of Grace's wedding, "*I* could have married her."[14]

THE J+M LIFE LESSON—MAINTAIN YOUR CENTER

When it came to men, when it came to almost anything, Jackie was a pretty cool customer—which was largely to her advantage. She maintained her center while dating, while Mari-

. . . .

14 To wrap up: Years later, when JFK was in the White House, Princess Grace of Monaco and her husband came to visit, and boy, did Jackie not like that idea. For starters, she downgraded her visit from a dinner to a luncheon (considered a dis). Pictures of the day show GK looking on quite adoringly at JFK.

lyn had a tendency to go off the deep end a bit (well, she was an actress) or at least to fall madly in love with the wrong guy.

Marilyn, unlike Jackie, wore her heart on her sleeve and then some. If she was upset over something, the world was going to know about it, and she was perfectly capable of taking to her bed for days on end.

When Johnny Hyde died, she managed to push her way into his funeral—against the wishes of his family—and threw herself over his coffin, weeping.

Wow. A young, beautiful twentysomething MM (perfectly coiffed and dressed in black, of course) draping herself over your coffin. Most men would dream of a send-off like that. Only in Hollywood, right?

But she was authentically bereft at the loss of her dear friend.

Jackie, on the other hand—like the Kennedy and Onassis families—watched the angles. She was far more capable of looking analytically at any situation, even *l'affaire d'amour.* If she was in a situation where the ship was about to go down, she wasn't going to be on it.

THE END OF THE AFFAIR

For whatever reason, you and Mr. Wonderful have decided to call it quits. Now is the time that you really want to channel Jackie and do a slow (if elegant) fade-out. Your heart may be broken, you might have a million questions you *must* ask him. You miss him and all the fun times you had together. . . .

So what (as JKO would advise with her usual brand of soigné toughness).

The main thing is this: Do not turn into Stalker Chick. Do not ask him to "explain himself." Boring. If you aren't happy, that is enough of a reason to leave.

Do not send him emails.

Take him off your Facebook friend list (not that he should have been on it in the first place).

Delete his number from your cell phone.

Do not send him news articles you think he might be interested in.

The fact that he is never going to see you again is enough of a psychic price to pay. You don't need to inflict any more drama or heartache on the guy.

Gone is gone.

SECRET SECRETS—THE JACKIE: THINGS YOU MIGHT NOT KNOW ABOUT HER

Perhaps it was the supersocial world she grew up in, but Jackie always loved going on dates. She also made each of her escorts feel as if he was the most fascinating man on earth.

SECRET SECRETS—THE MARILYN: THINGS YOU MIGHT NOT KNOW ABOUT HER

As a young Hollywood starlet, MM had no problems scheduling three dates in an evening (with three separate admirers): cocktails, dinner and après-dinner late-night clubbing.

"I don't think there are any men who are faithful to their wives."

— JKO

. . . .

"Marriage is my main career from now on."

— MM

In marriage, Jackie and Marilyn aimed high. Although Jackie seemed far more interested in the social aspects of marriage (as compared to Marilyn), since that was the world she was raised in, she did not go for the typical WASP stockbroker who played golf on the weekends and bitched about paying taxes. They both went for the smartest, most creative, best-looking man in the room.[1] Marilyn, for her part, conjured up the near impossible in her last marriage—a Pulitzer Prize–winning playwright/tough guy from Brooklyn who could also use his fists and look good in a white T-shirt (in a craggy, Lincoln-esque sort of way).

When push came to shove, neither Jackie nor Marilyn[2] set-

. . . .

1 Or more likely, the smartest, most creative, best-looking man in the room went for them.
2 With the exception of MM's first marriage, when she had no other options.

tled. Simple put: They married the man at the top of the heap whom they were madly in love with. And remember Joan's ultimate put-down of a guy on *Mad Men*? "He reminds me of a *doorman*."

That was not the man they chose.

In thinking about who they married, Jackie probably went for power (in the social, political and financial field), while Marilyn went for talent (in writing, in baseball), although the distinction may be somewhat moot, since talent often brings power, and power can come from talent. At any rate, Jackie and Marilyn (and again, it may have been more unconscious on her part) went for the name brand when choosing a life partner.

MARILYN'S STARTER MARRIAGE

Her first, to James Dougherty, was literally a child bride situation. Married off just days past her sixteenth birthday, because it was either that or go back into yet another foster home, the marriage was—like Marilyn at that time—nebulous from the start.

Marilyn and Jimmy, officially husband and wife, lived almost like brother and sister. When he went away to the war, leaving her alone—and there are some women you simply do not leave alone—Marilyn was discovered by Army photographer David Conover while working in a parachute factory in 1945, and the die was cast.

From the start, the camera loved Marilyn. A lonely child, docile, well behaved, "pretty good" at school (but nothing exceptional like Jackie), with an absent mother and shunted from foster home to foster home, she came alive in front of a camera. Looking at her early test shots before she became the Marilyn of millions of men's dreams, even in her struggling anonymity, it is no small thing to say that the camera loved her.

And it did.

Marilyn came alive for the camera in a way that she rarely did for her first husband. Years later, after she had moved into the stratosphere of celebrity far, far past him, Dougherty turned bitter, remembering the simple, loving girl who now sang for a president, had married one of the gods of baseball. "Marilyn had no problem being married as long as I could do something for her," he recalled. He was small-minded and petty, something MM (for all of her faults) never was.

MARILYN AND THE YANKEE CLIPPER

Her second marriage captured America's imagination.

At first, she did not even want to meet baseball great Joe DiMaggio—knowing nothing about sports, she wondered what they would even talk about. But he had seen her photograph in the newspaper and insisted on an introduction.

When they first met in a restaurant, Marilyn found him quiet, respectful, not at all the athlete show-off she expected. They grew close, and after dating for two years were married by a San Francisco justice of the peace on January 14, 1954, surrounded by a scrum of reporters and fans, although they tried to keep it quiet.

Like the rest of America, Marilyn's bosses at Fox were delighted with the union. "We didn't lose an actress," they said, "we gained a center fielder."

In spite of the inherent romance of their union—the baseball star and the pinup girl—there were fundamental problems from the start. DiMaggio's career was winding down, and he wanted Monroe to stay home and be less Marilyn and more Mrs. Joe DiMaggio. And for a time, it seemed, she tried.

DiMaggio was supposed to be remarkable in bed, which always helps. Unfortunately, there was the life they had to lead outside the bedroom—it always comes to that eventually, doesn't it? They loved each other. They just could not live together. Marilyn wanted to be an ordinary housewife, she really did—to stay home nights and watch television, the way Joe liked. Now that she was Mrs. Joe DiMaggio, he expected her to tone down her "Marilyn-ness"—that thing that attracted him to her in the first place. Don't dress so sexy, don't drive other men wild. Give up your career. She learned to cook a good Italian red sauce from his mother. She befriended, even loved, his son from his first marriage, Joe Junior. (Years later, he remembered that she used to write him letters posing as one of the family dogs, saying that she had been chewing things up.)

But still, demure cotton blouses buttoned up to her chin and Italian red sauce aside, she was *Marilyn,* and the cameras and the studios and her future beckoned. What did he expect? What did any husband of hers expect?

The famous sidewalk scene in *The Seven Year Itch* was the nail in their marital coffin (so to speak).

It was a night shoot in New York City, Lexington and 52nd. The Fox publicists had alerted the newspaper columnists that Marilyn would be wearing something that "would really stop traffic," and somehow the entire city seemed to know that Marilyn was in town, shooting a movie on the East Side. There was Marilyn, luminous, in a plunging, deeply cut V-neck dress, no stockings and two pairs of white panties, it was said, to get around the censor. The crowd—thousands of anonymous men, it seemed, hovering, as ravenous as any wolf pack, waited on Marilyn's every move.

It was a scene Joltin' Joe—famously jealous to begin with—never should have seen.

The lights were ready. The cameras were in place. The wind machine, sadistically positioned under the subway grating, too, was in place. Marilyn and her costar, Tom Ewell, walked over it again and again and again.

The crowd howled. Marilyn smiled and held the hem of her dress down the best she could, then turned and posed prettily. She almost couldn't help herself. If the men loved her (and there was no doubt that they did), the camera loved her more.

She laughed, she giggled. She threw back her head and held the word's attention as she struggled (but not really) to keep her dress from blowing above her waist. You could also tell: She *loved* it.

Joe was seething. He and Walter Winchell had begun the evening at Toots Shors . . . and now this disgrace?—god-*dammit!* No wife of his should ever behave like this!

Seemingly unable to separate life from art (and who could blame him, really?) Joe had words with Marilyn, had words with Billy Wilder, had a fit and stormed off the set.

Later that night, he and Marilyn argued at their hotel and, it is said, he hit her.

They went back to California and tried to rebuild their marriage, but it was no use. Less than nine months later, on October 27, 1954, they were divorced.

MARILYN AND THE MAN WHO SOLD HER OUT

On June 29, 1956, Monroe married her third husband, playwright Arthur Miller, whom she had first met in 1950. Raised nominally as a Christian Scientist, she converted to Judaism for the ceremony.

Just prior to their marriage, Miller was called before the House Un-American Activities Committee (HUAC), a congressional committee that was investigating supposed communists working in Hollywood. Marilyn accompanied Miller to his testimony, putting her own career in jeopardy, and was beside him the entire time. Although it was not known at the time, she also paid for Miller's lawyers, as well as his alimony and child-support payments to his first wife, Mary Slattery.

Although we are sure there must have been love at the beginning of their relationship, maybe Marilyn was just too much for Miller to handle . . . or maybe it was the difficulties of two very creative people trying to live together. At any rate, Miller was mean to Marilyn, putting her down, mostly, for her lack of intellectual heft, versus his intellectual plaudits as the playwright of his generation. Shortly after their marriage, he began work on what would become *The Misfits,* and in spite of her extraordinarily compelling performance, Miller said that working on that project was the "lowest point" of his life. Shortly after the film commenced shooting, the pair separated.

Marilyn went to Mexico and got divorced from him on the day of Kennedy's inauguration on the advice of her publicist, Pat Newcomb, who thought the news of the world would be focused on Washington, D.C. It was.

Nineteen months later, Marilyn was dead from an apparently accidental drug overdose.

In the coming years, Miller really went to town on his relationship with one of the most famous women in the world. In 1964, he published *After the Fall,* a play about MM. And although it was known that he would not discuss his relationship with Marilyn, he wrote about her in great detail in his 1987 autobiography, *Timebends.* In each case, his characterization of MM was thought to be unnecessarily cruel.

But what was it Joan Didion wrote? "[There] is one last thing to remember: writers are always selling somebody out."

JACKIE AND JFK

"God, she loved Jack."

—C.Z. GUEST

Jackie and Senator John F. Kennedy were introduced at a dinner party at the home of their mutual friend Charles Bartlett in Georgetown. "We were introduced over the asparagus," Kennedy recalled. "They didn't serve asparagus," Jackie replied.

Although attracted to each other, they had what Jackie described as a "spasmodic" courtship and did not even see each other until six months after that first meeting.

Still, they both knew—on some level—that they had met their match.

Later, writing of herself in an authorized biography published when she was in the White House, Jackie described meeting Kennedy: "She knew instantly that he would have a profound, perhaps disturbing influence on her life. In a flash of inner perception, she realized that here was a man who did not want to marry. She was frightened. Jacqueline, in the revealing moment, envisaged heartbreak, but just as swiftly determined that heartbreak would be worth the pain."

And so it began.

Jack and Jackie were almost two halves of the same whole; even their names matched. Equally intelligent, ambitious, seductive, funny and hidden, both shied away from public displays of affection, and they were two of the most emotionally reserved people their mutual friend Ben Bradlee had ever met. At the same time, neither was a shrinking violet (though Jackie could be shy around people she did not know), and each was used to getting his or her own way.

So there would be sparks in their relationship.

As a rich man's son (and an Irish man with no interest in navel gazing or introspection), JFK probably did not foresee this possibility, but Jackie knew their similar personalities would cause some friction. "Since Jack is such a violently independent person, and I, too, am so independent, this marriage will take a lot of working out."

In retrospect, it is incredible how much they experienced together in their ten years of marriage. Almost immediately after their honeymoon, JFK returned to politics and threw himself into running for higher office. After serving in the Senate, his name was unexpectedly put on the ballot for vice president during the 1956 Democratic convention. While he did not win, he began to have national appeal. Running for reelection in the Senate and then for the presidency was grueling. When he won the 1960 election against Richard Nixon, Kennedy was, at forty-three, the youngest man ever elected president.

During these years, Kennedy also underwent a horrific back operation that almost killed him, authored a book (with Jackie's help), *Profiles in Courage,* that won a Pulitzer, and traveled the country, giving hundreds of speeches.

During his administration, he dealt with conflicts including the Bay of Pigs invasion, the Cuban missile crisis, the cold war, the construction of the Berlin Wall, and the beginning of what would become the Vietnam War. JFK also started the Peace Corps, introduced the importance of the arts to American society, and—with Jackie's help—elevated America's status abroad.

In their personal lives, there was tragedy and joy—Jackie gave birth to four children, Arabella (who died at birth), Caroline, John Junior, and Patrick (who lived just two days before dying of a lung ailment). Jackie's beloved father died, and JFK's father, the patriarch of the Kennedy family, suffered a crippling stroke.

And all of these events played out very much in the public sphere, with newsmen, and the world, watching their every move.

So yes, Jackie was right in thinking that meeting John F. Kennedy would have a "profound" influence on her life.

By the time they celebrated their ten-year anniversary, in September 1963, Jack and Jackie had been through so much together. As Jackie's mother put it, "I can't think of two people who had packed more into ten years of marriage than they had. And I felt that with all their strains and stresses . . . [they] had eased to the point where they were terribly close to each other. . . . He appreciated her gifts and she worshipped him and appreciated his humor and kindness, and they really had fun together."

In the end, no one really knows what goes on between two people, particularly two people so much in the public eye, but this much is undisputed: Jackie loved her husband. In later years, after the trauma of his death had faded—although it probably never did, she just learned, on some level, to live with it—she would sometimes tell anecdotes about "Jack," keeping his memory alive.

But it is known that Jackie could never bear to look at his picture after his death, and much later she admitted that she had difficulty remembering his voice.

. . . .

NOVEMBER 22, 1963

. . . .

JFK's assassination was the 9/11 of our parents'—or grandparents'—generation. After his death, Camelot was over. Jackie left Georgetown for the relative anonymity of New York City—too many memories of N Street and her "crooked little house." Grown men walked around shattered for months. Some—his brother, Bobby, his best friend, Lem Billings—never got over it. Marriages blew up, friendships ended. Some people never spoke to otherwise close friends again. It was as if JFK—the center of it all—was gone. And there was nothing holding them together anymore.

THE MYTH OF THE KENNEDY-MONROE ROMANCE

In one of the most famous (or infamous) love triangles of our time, there was Jackie, Marilyn and at the center, JFK.[3]

As one woman who knew him said, "Some men give off light and some men give off heat. He gave off light." Everyone loved JFK: old people, young people, dogs (although he was allergic to dogs and horses), egghead intellectuals, nuns. Everyone.

He was one of those men, largely neglected in childhood in favor of an overbearing older brother, Joe Junior, who had to depend on his personality and intellect to get attention. (Even now, men who knew him and worked in his administration get upset thinking about the loss. "Oh Christ, we loved Jack," one admits, finally, trying to explain it all.)

JFK—even his nickname, redolent of the can-do optimism of the 1960s, moved fast. He walked fast. His mind worked fast. He was a known speed reader who almost seemed to be in a race against time, against some future he could not imagine. He rarely planned ahead. He hated to be kept waiting on a date—or for anything.

The number, the scope and range of the women he dated was notable. Just in Hollywood, there was Angie Dickinson, Audrey Hepburn, Gene Tierney, Jayne Mansfield, Gypsy Rose Lee, his sister-in-law Lee Radziwill (if gossips are believed). Not to mention any num-

- - - - - - - - - - - - -

3 And, as these famous-person romantic roundelays go, JFK was not the only man they shared, but he was the only one in which there was obvious overlap. In the Jackie/Marilyn love connection, there was also Marlon Brando (Marilyn had gotten involved with him first) and Frank Sinatra (again, Marilyn); but decades separated Jackie's involvement with the two men who had romanced Marilyn in her younger days.

ber of secretaries, stewardesses, starlets and New York City society girls from nice families.

Jackie and Marilyn: Is it possible that each wanted (on some level) what the other possessed?

In a perfect world, Jackie could loan Marilyn class and "a good background," which we know in today's PC world sounds *awful*. Marilyn could impart Jackie with some sex appeal (and perhaps confidence), a more public sense of humor and a general loosening up.

Tabloid historians say that Marilyn dreamed of becoming the next Mrs. Kennedy and moving into the White House. With Jackie's radar instinct, we have no doubt that she knew all about MM. She knew, in the abstract and often in the specific, about all her husband's women.

In reality, though, JFK and MM met only four times in their entire lives, always in the company of others. Jack had a soft spot for actresses going through a hard time. As president, he used to call Judy Garland and ask her to sing "Somewhere Over the Rainbow" for him once in a while. So the myth of a great Kennedy-Monroe romance is largely that: a myth. As someone who traveled in that world said, "The Secret Service would have known about it—the Secret Service knew *everything*."

THAT DRESS

"Happy Birthday, Mr. Pre-s-i-*dent*. . . ."—MM

"I can now retire from politics after having had 'Happy Birthday' sung to me in such a sweet, wholesome way."—JFK

Let's pause for a moment to discuss the iconographic public moment JFK and MM shared that made people stop and wonder: *What?*

Imagine this happening today: a fund-raiser for the president of the United States, ostensibly celebrating his birthday, attended by more than 15,000 supporters at Madison Square Garden in New York City. Hosted by Jack Benny, the entertainment includes Peter Lawford, Marilyn Monroe, and a host of stars, including Maria Callas, Ella Fitzgerald, Jimmy Durante, Shirley MacLaine and Peggy Lee.

Putting Marilyn aside for the moment, the JFK birthday bacchanal is notable for its high jinks. And you realize that in the days before CNN, YouTube, twitter and 24/7 surveillance, *these people had fun.*

And best of all, they (the richies, Hollywood people, celebrities, Kennedys) didn't care who knew it.

Perhaps the largest political stag party in history, the event was actually televised on CBS, and it is wild to watch now. Picture it: Late night, May 19, 1962, we see the president of the United States smoking a cigar with his feet up on the parterre, clapping appreciatively to an actress—well, one of the actresses—he was rumored to be having an affair with, not caring who saw.[4]

JFK's "I don't give a damn" attitude is pretty fabulous. He is totally old school—sort of like everyone's dad of a previous generation. He just doesn't care, especially when you consider that his seventy-two-year-old mother and two sisters are in the audience with him. (Jackie is nowhere to be seen, having taken the children and decamped to Virginia and her horses in a snit.) It's very *Mad Men*. Actually, it is beyond *Mad Men*—it is how Don Draper would behave if he were

---

4 A fact not known by the general public at the time, obviously. (Not that anyone would have believed it anyway.)

the most powerful man in the world and not just a square-jawed ad exec.

Now, the dress. Monroe's dress (designed and made by Hollywood couturier Jean Louis at a cost of $11,000) was flesh colored with 2,500 rhinestones sewn into it. Adlai Stevenson described it as "skin and beads."

So form fitting that she had to be sewn into it, Marilyn did not (as was her wont) wear anything underneath it. She walked onstage and dropped the white fur coat, her hair, skin, gown and very much in evidence body bathed in an aura of light, and people gasped.

"Happy birth . . . day . . . to you . . ." she began tentatively. The children's tune turned into a seduction. The crowd—sounding like mostly men at a fight match—roared with disbelief at what they were seeing. It was such a blatant display of sexual pandemonium manifested in one woman.

Having paid $1,000 for her own ticket, it was Marilyn's last public performance.

For JFK's next (and final) birthday the following year, the anti-Marilyn, Audrey Hepburn, sang "Happy Birthday" to him.

And the dress? Marilyn's dress was sold at auction in 1999 for $1.3 million, one of the highest amounts of money ever paid for an article of clothing.

JACKIE AND ARISTOTLE ONASSIS

Aristotle Onassis, like JFK, like Joseph P. Kennedy, like "Black Jack" Bouvier, was a pirate. One of the original jet-setters (when the term meant something), he roamed the world, bending it to his will. As Napoleon said, "Circumstances— what are circumstances? I create circumstances."

One might say Jackie had a type.

. . . .

*B*orn in 1900, he made his first million importing tobacco in Argentina and quickly got into the oil and shipping business. From there, he became one of the wealthiest men in the world, going on to own more than seventy vessels, as well as stock in oil companies in the United States, the Middle East, and Venezuela. He also owned an airline (Olympic Airlines), a yacht (the *Christina*), two islands (Scorpios and Sparta), a gold-processing plant in Latin America, and lots of real estate—with apartments in Paris, London, Monte Carlo, Athens and Acapulco, and a castle in the south of France. In Manhattan, although he generally stayed at his suite at the Pierre, he owned a fifty-two-story high-rise called Olympic Tower, as well as a building on Sutton Place.

Onassis was not conventionally handsome, and did not photograph well. Yes, there was the money (which no doubt attracted Jackie, but there are a lot of rich guys in the world). But there was something about his energy. He had the world's dark magic. He was devastating to women. He had that trick of the professional seducer: He focused all of his attention on a woman, remembering everything she said, as well as her favorite flower, favorite perfume, favorite style of jewelry. Hélène Arpels, a Parisian socialite who knew him in the 1940s, well before he ascended to billionaire status, said that he was one of the most charismatic men she had ever met in her life.

He picked up the telephone, and things happened.

In many ways, Onassis was the anti-JFK.

He had considerable charm, but he was not an establishment smoothie. He was not formally educated but a genius in business; and you knew going into it, if you had any sense at all, that he was going to gain the upper hand in any dealings you might have with him. Like all great businessmen (like all those who hold our attention), he had the essential capacity for heartlessness.[5] He could be dismissive of his children. He ran

. . . .

5 What was it Balzac said? "Behind every great fortune there is a crime."

through people, treating Maria Callas, the great love of his life, abominably, tossing her aside, quite publicly, for Jackie.

When Jackie married Onassis on October 20, 1968, it was almost as if she had offended the world's sensibilities. "Jackie, How Could You?" read the headline of one newspaper, as Mrs. Kennedy, the beloved widow of JFK, became "Jackie O," the most famous woman in the world. For her part, Lee Radziwill probably called it right when she commented on the snobbishness by saying: "If Jackie's new husband had been blond, rich, young, and Anglo-Saxon, most Americans would have been much happier."

In the beginning (like so many things), all was fine in the House of Onassis. Jackie was a wonderful spouse. She learned Greek, refurbished Scorpios, doted on Ari as they traveled the world together. By all accounts, he took very good care of her and had a wonderful relationship with her children.

Then, cracks began to appear in their relationship. Onassis balked at Jackie's incessant spending. The accountants in his office began to call her "the supertanker" as the financial demands of maintaining her lifestyle cost Ari as much as one of his ships. (But still, said an associate of Onassis's, "I'm sure he was no picnic to live with either.") They grew apart as Jackie spent more time in New York City and Ari in Greece, Paris or London.

The end of the relationship occurred on January 24, 1973, when Onassis's only son, Alexander, was killed in an airplane crash. He was twenty-five years old. His son's tragic death dealt Onassis a shattering blow from which he never recovered. Although Jackie tried to be supportive, Onassis's grief was so intense, so unrelenting, that he went a little mad. Veering wildly between bouts of depression and rage, he spoke of divorce and spent hours obsessively reworking his will. Before any of this could take place, he died, in Paris, on March 15, 1975.

MRS. O'S SHOPPING ALLOWANCE

For all the men who gripe about their wives' extravagant spending; well, it could be a lot worse. You could have been married to Jackie—who had no qualms about spending ten minutes in a store and running up a $50,000 tab. Every day.

And although he had a fortune estimated at $500 million to $1 billion (in 1969 dollars) and had no problem buying Jackie some major baubles (among his gifts to his wife were a $1.25-million heart-shaped, ruby-and-diamond engagement ring and a $1-million 40.42-carat diamond ring from Cartier for her fortieth birthday), Onassis eventually became enraged by Jackie's prodigious shopping.

The couple's arguments over money escalated, their differences grew more apparent, and the two spent less and less time together. "They started with separate beds in the same bedroom," Onassis's colleague said, "and ended with separate beds on separate continents."

THE JACKIE LIFE LESSON—LEARN TO OVERLOOK THE SMALL STUFF

If there is anything Jackie learned in her marriages to two high-powered men, it was to overlook the small stuff.

During her ten-year marriage to JFK, there had been so much real drama: being drawn into the very public Kennedy family whirlwind, a life she did not grow up aspiring to lead; two miscarriages and the sorrowful deaths of two babies, Arabella and Patrick; JFK's hidden illnesses (he was given the Last Rites of the Catholic Church three times before the age of forty); JFK's run for the presidency and winning by one of the smallest margins in U.S. history; the death of her beloved father at the age of sixty-six; and on and on and on. It almost didn't make sense to bitch about the things most couples squabbled about, like: What are we going to watch on television tonight?

Between JFK's death and her marriage to Aristotle Onassis in 1968, there were the assassinations of Robert F. Kennedy and Martin Luther King, Jr., the escalation of the war in Vietnam, the increasing violence in the streets of America. And while her marriage to Onassis brought her unimaginable material comforts, she lost most of her privacy and, at times, could barely walk out her front door without being besieged by paparazzi.

By the time she hit her sixties, she had been through so much trauma and heartbreak that she became very zen about her experiences.

Jackie was more apt to laugh at people's foibles or the sense that one "should" do something, which made her clash with her mother, Janet Auchincloss (who felt very strongly about what "should" be done and made sure Jackie knew it[6]) and mother-in-law, Rose Kennedy. In one famous instance, Rose told Jackie that they were expecting important guests for lunch and to make sure that she was at the table on time. Jackie did not come downstairs at all. Instead, she remained in bed and, in fact, had a maid bring her lunch up on a tray.

In spite of her regal public demeanor she was, inside, a free spirit—much like her father, "Black Jack" Bouvier, or her nutty aunt and cousin "Big Edie" and "Little Edie" Beale.[7] John H. Davis, a cousin who wrote *The Bouviers* in 1993, described her as a young woman who outwardly seemed to conform to social norms. But he wrote that she possessed a "fiercely independent inner life which she shared with few people and would one day be partly responsible for her enormous success."

What we're saying is this: Pick your battles. Don't make everything into World War III. Occasionally, you can pull a Jackie and sulk (which drove JFK nuts), or if your man's done something that really annoys you, either put it on the table and discuss it or disappear for a while.

That will get his attention.

. . . .

6 When she was in the White House, Mrs. Auchincloss was always telling her daughter that her hair was too "messy" and "windblown."
7 Of *Grey Gardens* fame.

In today's world, we would suggest that you learn to let things slide once in a while. When your significant other says (or does) something really irritating but excusable, be like JKO and ignore it. He might be testing you, or he might just be bored.

THE ART OF CONVERSATION

There was one thing both Jackie and Marilyn were experts at, and that is holding a man's attention through the art of conversation . . . although to be honest, they each had to say very little in terms of actual *sentences* to get someone's attention—it was more the *way* they might say something.

(One thinks, here, of a famous dinner party at Peter and Pat Lawford's home in Santa Monica in 1962, where Marilyn met then–Attorney General Robert F. Kennedy. She wanted to have a conversation about civil rights and pulled out a piece of paper with her questions written out in lipstick—which, you have to admit, for an opening gambit was pretty original, even for Marilyn. Kennedy was charmed and spent the rest of the evening speaking to her.)

One of the first things that attracted JFK to Jackie was her intelligence. During their courtship, when she was put through the ringer of a Kennedy family weekend (word games: yes; touch football: not so much), JFK soon learned to get her on his team during hard-fought battles of charades, as her side invariably won. After they were married, many of the best lines from his speeches (whether from George Bernard Shaw or Yeats) were often supplied by the more literary Jackie.

. . . .
A Touch of Reality That No MM Movie Ever Touched Upon
. . . .

Has anyone noticed that American society fetishizes the wedding day without placing enough emphasis on the fact that now you are married to the guy and have to stay married?

Just saying.

CLOSING THE DEAL

. . . .

"Will You . . . ?"

. . . .

If you're a Jackie, Don't Say Yes Right Off the Bat. If You're a Marilyn, Don't Say Yes at All. The Luckiest Guy in the World has just proposed, and you might decide to burst into tears and start screaming, "Yes! Yes! Yes!" right away (like *The Bachelor*), or you might decide to go on a cruise and tell him you will consider it. In either event, it is a story you are going to have to tell your children (or, maybe, his children—your stepchildren), so make sure you maintain your dignity.[8]

*W*hen JFK asked Jackie to marry him after a year-long courtship, she agreed in principle, but then took off to cover Queen Elizabeth's coronation in London, letting him know that she needed to consider the reality of the whole Marrying a Kennedy thing.

Her coverage of the coronation appeared on

. . . .

8 It's not so much a delaying tactic as an "I need to think about it" tactic. If nothing else, it will show him (and the world) that you recognize the seriousness of what is about to take place.

the front page of the Washington newspapers, and JFK wired her: "article great but you are missed." When she returned to America, he surprised her by meeting her plane in Boston. And when they saw each other again in person, she officially agreed to become Mrs. Kennedy.

. . . .

THE CEREMONY

. . . .

If it is your first wedding, do whatever you want, and don't let your mother run the show—she had her day.[9] If it's your second, think tasteful. A Valentino daytime dress should do the trick.

Because of her celebrity and innate personal shyness (yes, really), Marilyn's second (to Joe DiMaggio) and third (to Arthur Miller) marriages were small small small. If you are a Marilyn, you want your marriage service as small as possible without offending your in-laws, whether it is your first or your third trip down the aisle. While there is no shame in a justice of the peace ceremony, don't go to Vegas.

COMPARING JKO'S AND MM'S FIRST WEDDINGS

"More than anything in the world," a friend remembered during Jackie's engagement to JFK in 1953, "Jackie wanted to be Mrs. John F. Kennedy."

Jackie's first wedding was not what she had in mind (tasteful, Newport chic), but instead was a giant Kennedy-palooza masterminded for maximum publicity by family patriarch Joseph P. Kennedy with twenty-four bridesmaids, a blessing from the cardinal and 1,200 in attendance, with the entire U.S. Senate invited.

. . . .

9 Not incidentally, JKO agreed with this. When her daughter, Caroline, married Edwin Schlossberg in 1986, she did not even want to see the wedding dress that Carolina Herrera designed, saying, "It's Caroline's day, whatever she wants."

It was a great society bash as guests sat at tables on the lawn, dined on creamed chicken, viewed the wedding gifts displayed in the house and danced to the Meyer Davis Orchestra on the terrace of Hammersmith Farm, the Auchincloss estate in Newport.

The night before, JFK gave a toast and joked that he had to marry Jackie to remove her from the Fourth Estate, because she was becoming too big a risk to his political fortunes. For her part, Jackie held up a postcard that Kennedy, "a Pulitzer Prize–winning author," had sent her—his lone romantic missive throughout their courtship—and read it to the crowd: "Wish you were here. Jack"

En route to their honeymoon in Acapulco, Jackie wore a gray Chanel suit and a diamond feather brooch that was a wedding gift from her husband.

Marilyn's first wedding was a slapdash, almost haphazard affair. Her mother did not attend, and she did not know who her father was. At 8:30 on the evening of June 19, 1942, the ceremony was performed by a nondenominational minister named Benjamin Lingenfelder at the home of Mr. and Mrs. Chester Howell (friends of Grace's) at 432 South Bentley Avenue, West Los Angeles. Everything seemed slightly surreal and improvised. A girl Norma Jeane/Marilyn knew only slightly at University High was her matron of honor; Jim's brother Marion was best man. The groom recalled that Marilyn "was shaking so much she could hardly stand."

A modest reception was held at a nearby restaurant, where a showgirl entertaining another wedding party dragged Dougherty onto a makeshift stage for a dance. But when he returned to his table, he found his bride "not very happy." She thought he had "made a monkey" out of himself.

At about four in the morning, the newlyweds returned home to Sherman Oaks. There was no honeymoon.

Are DIAMONDS A GIRL'S BEST FRIEND?

To be honest, the Kennedys were not big on what they considered extraneous expenses. They would spend money—lots of it—to get one of the boys elected to the presidency or the Senate, but they didn't spend much on antiques, artwork, jewelry, fixing the roof or paying the help a decent wage. Jackie had a very nice 2.8-carat emerald and diamond engagement ring from Van Cleef & Arpels (picked out and paid for by Kennedy père, Joseph P. Kennedy) and a Schlumberger brooch that her husband bought her after their son, John, was born. But mostly she wore costume jewelry—pearl necklaces bought at Bergdorf Goodman for about $35 in the 1950s[10] and faux diamond earrings.

Jackie didn't have any real jewelry prior to the go-go Onassis years—and what years they were, jewelry-wise. In the early, happy years of their courtship and marriage, Onassis got into the habit of giving JKO a little something on her breakfast tray. There was a 40-carat diamond engagement ring (later bought by Irish millionaire Tony O'Reilly for his wife for $2.5 million at the Sotheby's auction after her death) that JKO wore twice and otherwise kept in a safe deposit box in New York, a 20-carat ruby ring, a pair of cabochon ruby and diamond ear clips and matching pendant—which were a wedding gift from Onassis in 1968.

As Maria Callas said of Onassis, "Anything he learned about women he learned from a Van Cleef & Arpels catalogue."

Which, you have to admit, is not a bad way to go.

THE END GAME

After a marriage had ended (through tragedy and death in each of Jackie's two marriages, and divorce in Marilyn's), Jackie and Marilyn always spoke lovingly of their husbands.

---

10 After her death, two faux pearl necklaces worn by JKO were sold for $112,500 at the Sotheby's auction.

In spite of JFK's rumored infidelities (which never became public during his lifetime), Jackie never spoke of him less than lovingly. "Now he is a legend when he would have preferred to be a man."

After Onassis's death, regardless of the fact that the jet set was buzzing with rumors that the Kennedy-Onassis marriage was on its last legs, Jackie remembered her time with him gracefully: "Aristotle Onassis rescued me at a moment when my life was engulfed with shadows. . . . He brought me into a world where one could find both happiness and love. We lived through many beautiful experiences together which cannot be forgotten and for which I will be eternally grateful."

To friends, she told funny stories about how Ari was an insomniac and would go for walks up Park Avenue at all hours of the night and drag friends home with him.

After her divorce from Arthur Miller, Monroe spoke of the split with dignity, saying to reporters, "It would be indelicate of me to discuss this. I feel it would be trespassing. Mr. Miller is a wonderful man and a great writer, but it didn't work out that we should be husband and wife. But everybody I ever loved, I still love a little."

Ending a marriage or a long-term relationship is always painful. From Jackie and Marilyn's example, we have one thing to say: Take the high road. Always. Because at one point, you loved him enough to marry him. And there may be children involved, and if not children, then in-laws and a whole constellation of friends and family members surrounding you.

And besides (as Jackie and Marilyn knew), the way you speak of someone says more about you than him.

POSTSCRIPT

At the very end, Joe DiMaggio tried to be Marilyn's protector. At the time of her death, on August 5, 1962, she and Joe DiMaggio were planning on remarrying just four days later. Joe DiMaggio hated Hollywood, hated the hustlers and the agents and the schemers and the yes men who (he felt) had all contributed to Marilyn's death.

The day after her death, her body—desired by millions—lay at the Los Angeles County Morgue, with no family member to claim it. DiMaggio stepped in. He called Allan "Whitey" Snyder, Monroe's friend and longtime makeup man, to make sure that Marilyn looked her best. Ten years earlier, she had secured a promise from him: "Promise me that if anything happens to me—please, nobody must touch my face but you. Promise me you'll do my makeup, so I'll look my best when I leave."

"Sure," he said, laughing, kidding around, "but bring the body back while it's still warm and I'll do it."

A few weeks later, Allen received a gift from Marilyn in a sky blue Tiffany box—a gold money clip with the engraving: "Whitey dear—While I'm still warm—Marilyn."

And so he fulfilled his last promise to her.

DiMaggio took control of her funeral, allowing only thirty relatives and friends to attend—no studio executives, no producers, no Hollywood stars (and god knows, no newsmen, photographers or reporters). Her acting coach, Lee Strasberg, spoke briefly: "We knew her as a warm human being, impulsive, shy and lonely, sensitive and in fear of rejection, yet ever avid for life and for reaching out for fulfillment. The dream of her talent was not a mirage."

Years earlier, Marilyn had told DiMaggio the story of William Powell's pledge to the dying Jean Harlow—that he would deliver flowers to her grave and not forget her. Knowing how moved Marilyn was by this story, he had a bouquet of roses delivered to her crypt three times a week for the next twenty years. He never wrote or spoke publicly of their relationship. Nor did he remarry. According to his son, he never got over her death. It is said that his final words were, "I'll finally get to see Marilyn."

WOULD SHE DO IT AGAIN?

Twice widowed by the age of forty-five, Jacqueline would not marry again. "I have always lived through men," she confided to a friend after Onassis's death. "Now I realize I can't do that anymore." In the 1970s, as an editor at Doubleday involved in an extremely settled and happy relationship with Maurice Tempelsman, Jackie once said that if she had to do it all over again, she might have stayed single and been a globe-trotting journalist like her friend Gloria Emerson.

SECRET SECRETS — THE MARILYN:
THINGS YOU MIGHT NOT KNOW ABOUT HER

Although their marriage ended badly, Marilyn kept every letter that Arthur Miller ever wrote her.

SECRET SECRETS — THE JACKIE:
THINGS YOU MIGHT NOT KNOW ABOUT HER

Prior to her marriage, Jackie (like all of her family and pretty much every single member of her social set) was a Republican. Marrying into the Kennedy clan, she knew she had to switch her allegiance to the Dems. And she did.

7 : *The Life of the Mind*

"He [Arthur Miller] wouldn't have married me if I had been nothing but a dumb blonde."

—MM

. . . .

"I always wanted to be some kind of a writer. . . . Like a lot of people, I dreamed of writing the Great American Novel."

—JKO

*Sex*pots read Nietzsche, too, you know. Diana Vreeland, the legendary style maker and *Vogue* editor (and friend of both Jackie's and Marilyn's) had it right when she said, "The only real elegance is in the mind; if you've got that, the rest really comes from it."[1]

And while they were both stylish and visually compelling women, Jackie and Marilyn took this insight to heart, knowing that no matter how pretty one might be, it was what went on inside that made her memorable.

. . . .

1 DV was friends with both Jackie and Marilyn. She advised JBK on her inaugural ensembles in 1961 and also commissioned a famous *Vogue* shoot with Bert Stern and MM in 1962.

JACKIE'S SCHOOL DAYS

As a young woman of privilege, Jackie received the best education in the country. Able to read before grammar school, she attended Miss Chapin's School on East End Avenue in New York City. Bright, rambunctious and sometimes bored, she acted up and often found herself in the office of headmistress Ethel Stringfellow. Miss Stringfellow got her to focus and direct her talent by comparing her to a thoroughbred, saying that "without self-discipline and training, the horse's abilities would serve no use." She later recalled that "I mightn't have kept Jacqueline, except that she had the most inquiring mind we'd had in the school in thirty-five years." The headmistress's redirection worked.

From there, Jackie went to Miss Porter's School, an all-girls' boarding school in Farmington, Connecticut. Jackie was well liked at Farmington (in the preppie parlance of the day) and made some lifelong friendships—among them Nancy Tuckerman ("Tucky"), who would not only work with her in the White House but for most of the remainder of her adult life. Well liked and popular, her teachers regarded her as an outstanding student, but she once fretted to a friend, "I'm sure no one will ever marry me, and I'll end up being a housemother at Farmington."

Jackie attended Vassar for two years, and while she loved it intellectually, she began to chafe at being stuck up in Poughkeepsie, referring to it as "that damn Vassar." When the opportunity arose to study at the Sorbonne in Paris during her junior year, she jumped at it. Later, she recalled that it was "the happiest time of my life." Since there was no way that she was going back to Vassar, she ended her college career at George Washington University in Washington, D.C., graduating with a bachelor's degree in French literature.

Although she might have hidden it during her early dating forays, Jackie was smart. Jackie was always smart. She knew a lot, and then she wanted to know more.

Unlike the typical mind-set that led to a calcified worldview as one gets older, Jackie was always, always pushing for new books, new experiences, new people, new thoughts. A friend who knew her says, "Jackie wasn't an intellectual, but she made the effort to find out what was going on in the world." When she was in the White House, she made Oleg Cassini show everyone how to do "the twist," a new dance craze that was sweeping New York City. Throughout her life, if there was a painter, a poet or a writer she admired, she might write him or her a fan letter, and they often became friends. In the 1970s, she met *New Yorker* cartoonist Charles Addams this way.

Moving beyond the casual, comfortable prejudices of the 1940s Newport she grew up in (against the blacks, Jews, Catholics, Irish—pretty much any non-WASP), by the end of her life Jackie was doing yoga and meditating, working at a "real" job, and mixing with people from all kinds of backgrounds.

Once on the beach at Skorpios, she had a conversation with her friend Vivian Crespi. "Do you realize how lucky we are, Vivi? To have gotten out of that world we came from. . . . Going every day to that club with the same kinds of people. . . . You and I have taken such a big bite out of life."

MARILYN'S EDUCATION

Marilyn's education (much like her upbringing) was the complete opposite of Jackie's. She got none of the praise that went with being the brightest girl in the class. She did not spend hours in her beautiful yellow and white bedroom overlooking Narragansett Sound, reading Shakespeare.

Instead, Marilyn (then Norma Jeane) went to local public schools in Los Angeles. She attended Emerson Junior High School in West Los Angeles, between Wilshire and Santa Monica boulevards. At school she was mostly anonymous and did not really stand out as a student. Her courses were designed for girls not on the college track—science, office practice, English, bookkeeping. She received mostly B's and C's. As she recalled,

"I loved English. I hated arithmetic. I was always staring out the window."

"She was very much an average student," recalled Mabel Ella Campbell, who taught the life sciences class. "But she looked as though she wasn't well cared for. Her clothes separated her a little bit from the rest of the girls. . . . Norma Jeane was a nice child, but not at all outgoing, not vibrant."

She went to Van Nuys High School, where her report card was even less distinguished than at junior high. For the second half of her sophomore year, she attended University High School at the corner of Westgate and Texas avenues. By this time, the fifteen-year-old had begun to date Jim Dougherty, a handsome neighbor five years her senior. In mid-March, she shocked her teachers and classmates by informing them that she was quitting school to get married in June 1942. After that, she was not seen in class again, and her formal studies officially ended in the middle of her second year of high school.

In spite of her abysmal education, Marilyn, in her own way, also yearned to know. Although she did not have Jackie's impressive pedigree, she was always reading and going to art galleries when she could and attending the occasional college course. Having already appeared in a few small but memorable roles in *Love Happy* (1949) with the Marx brothers and *The Asphalt Jungle*, directed by John Huston, she signed a seven-year contract with 20th Century

Fox the following year. It is telling that even at this early stage of her career, in 1951, she took evening courses at UCLA in "art appreciation and literature."

Later, as her career skyrocketed, it would be impossible for her to sit in a college classroom anonymously. In 1955 (after she became a star), she attended the famed Actors Studio in New York City and studied with Lee Strasberg.

Unlike most 21st-century Americans, she had a great desire for self-improvement. She kept a list of words that she was unfamiliar with and looked them up when she had a chance.

Marilyn had a touching belief in Merriam-Webster and the power of education.

ZEN AND THE ART OF ABSOLUTE FABULOUSNESS

. . . .

THE JACKIE PHILOSOPHY

. . . .

Jackie was outwardly religious and privately spiritual. Practicing her own highly individual form of Zen Catholicism, she often lit a candle in church for friends going through a tough time but then might also bake them a chocolate cake. Well versed in the tenets of the Catholic Church from the tragedies she endured—the untimely deaths of John F. Kennedy and Robert F. Kennedy, her miscarriages and the death of her son, Patrick, who lived only a few days, she thought "the Catholic Church understands death. . . . If it weren't for the children, we'd welcome it."

From JFK she learned to have (as he did) an almost fatalistic view of life that pushed against the Kennedy ethos that believed with enough money, enough power, enough hard work, enough juice, you could bend the outcome of events to your will. "It is not reality that counts," Joseph P. Kennedy counseled Jackie and his children, "it is the appearance that counts." Instead, JFK thought that whatever was going to happen was going to happen—and there was very little you could do about it. As

Jackie said, "From my husband I learned to do the best you can and then the hell with it."

From the Kennedys, Jackie also gained a sense of their fundamental joy in life, its lightness and humor; but also the senselessness of trying to control it and even the ridiculousness of planning for the future. So one should take whatever joy one might come across, whatever beauty or laughter, because there was often heartbreak lurking around the corner.

For Jackie to be able to fashion some sort of life for herself after November 22, 1963, she had to let a lot of things go: ignore them, not discuss them. Although she went to a psychiatrist once a week in the 1970s, she had no interest in reading the *Warren Report,* or finding out who killed her husband or following conspiracy theorists. "None of it will bring him back, will it?"

While Jackie was Catholic, she was also very drawn to India (which might have something to do with the fact that when she visited in 1961, crowds followed her, calling, "Ameriki Rani").[2] An interest in myths was furthered when she edited

. . . .
2 "Queen of America"

a book written by Bill Moyers, *The Power of Myth*.[3] In the 1980s, she meditated every evening from 7:00 to 7:30 and befriended Deepak Chopra. When he was in town, they even meditated together. "She had no ego," Chopra recalled. "She was very natural. She had a great sense of humor! She was a lot of fun, the way she joked and kidded around."

There was nothing mean-spirited about Jackie (well, only a little, in the service of a good punch line or to illustrate a point). She was a great conversationalist; the ability to tell a story, to hold a room, to make another human being laugh was no small thing. While her charm was as real as her smile, she also believed strongly in the adage "Never let the facts get in the way of a good story."

. . . .
THE MARILYN PHILOSOPHY
. . . .

Marilyn was more purely spiritual. If she had an ethos, it might have come from the Dalai Lama: "My religion is very simple. My religion is kindness."

Growing up, she had an "Aunt Grace," a friend of her mother's who helped raise her, named Grace McKee Goddard. She had an interest in Mary Baker Eddy and was one of the few people who were good to Marilyn. Goddard gave her a copy of *Science and Health With Key to the Scriptures,* and Marilyn kept it with her and read it throughout her life.

But Marilyn was fairly ecumenical. She also had a beautiful rosary made of large garnet beads and an oversized cross. It was a gift to her from Joe DiMaggio and had belonged to his mother. Marilyn used it often—the beads were worn down, like worry beads.[4]

Marilyn, far more than the emotionally circumspect Jackie, wore her heart on her sleeve. A true actress, her heart was sometimes a roller coaster of emotions—from laughter to tears,

. . . .

3 That nobody at Doubleday wanted to publish, BTW. It became a huge best seller.
4 It was mysteriously sold to a private collector for $50,000 in 2006.

often within minutes. She saw beauty in a sunset, a flower, one person's kindness to another, a child's laughter.

And just when you thought you had our two women figured out—that Jackie was the cool one and Marilyn the sexpot; Jackie the brains and Marilyn the beauty, there is this:

> *"I believe that everything happens for a reason.*
> *People change so that you can learn to let go,*
> *things go wrong so that you appreciate them*
> *when they're right, you believe lies so you*
> *eventually learn to trust no one but yourself,*
> *and sometimes good things fall apart so better*
> *things can fall together."*
>
> —MM

Not bad, right?

And the take-away (other than having this sentiment taped to your bathroom mirror so that you can read it every morning) for today's Marilyns? Take a tip from MM (as seen in some of her more memorable comedic screen roles like the *Seven Year Itch* and *Gentlemen Prefer Blondes*): When in doubt, say less than necessary.

JACKIE AND MARILYN DIDN'T JUDGE

In any event, both Jackie and Marilyn were extremely liberal when faced with the personal peccadilloes of others. They had certainly seen enough of the world and all of its vagaries not to judge. (Which is not to say that Jackie or Marilyn did not have opinions about people, about situations—in fact, Jackie believed, along with one of her favorite writers, Ernest Hemingway, that "action revealed character," and she *loved* hearing the inside scoop on all the people she knew. When she was in the White House, she saved her favorite Hollywood gossip she had heard and shared it with JFK to entertain him and take his mind off the complexities of the day.)

Jackie and Marilyn were each extremely open-minded when it came to the life choices of others. Her Vassar classmate Selwa Roosevelt remembered that Jackie "was discriminating in her tastes, not discriminatory towards people. In fact, she was always open to new ideas, new people and new ways of thinking."

JACKIE AND MARILYN STAY HOME WITH A GOOD BOOK

ON JACKIE'S BOOKSHELF

Jackie was always a reader. In an autobiographical essay about her childhood, she recalled, "I read a lot when I was little, much of which was too old for me. There were Chekhov and Shaw in the room where I took naps and I never slept but sat on the windowsill reading, then scrubbed the soles of my feet so the nurse would not see that I had been out of bed. My heroes were Byron, Mowgli, Robin Hood, Little Lord Fauntleroy's grandfather, and Scarlett O'Hara."

Her entire life, Jackie read everything—old stuff, new stuff, French existentialists, the *New York Post*. Between her various homes, she owned thousands of books, some bought, many that were gifts and signed by the author, first editions. Traveling across the country on the Kennedy family plane, the *Caroline*, on the campaign trail in 1961, she put her feet up and read a battered paperback copy of Jack Kerouac's *On the Road*. In India, she discovered the love poetry of Rumi, the brilliant 13th-century Persian mystic (a favorite of Audrey Hepburn's, too). At her place on Martha's Vineyard, one wall in her bedroom had a floor-to-ceiling bookcase filled exclusively with French literature.

She was also friendly with writers, and like a fan, invited such authors as Robert Lowell, William Styron and Mary Hemingway to the White House.[5]

Also on Jackie's bookshelf:

In the Russian Style (edited and with intro by JKO)

The White House: An Historic Guide (authored by JBK)

Unseen Versailles, Deborah Turbeville and Louis Auchincloss (edited by JKO)

Grand Central Terminal, Deborah Nevins (edited by JKO)

Present Indicative, Noël Coward

White House Nanny, Maud Shaw

Rose: A Biography of Rose Fitzgerald Kennedy, Gail Cameron

House of Splendid Isolation, Edna O'Brien (inscribed)

The Land of the Firebird, Suzanne Massie (inscribed)

Bound copies of *The Paris Review*

The Sunset of the Romanov Dynasty, inscribed by Suzanne Massie

Selected Poetry and Prose of William Blake

The Prodigal Rake, William Hickey

Pigeon Feathers and Other Stories, John Updike

Six Plays, Lillian Hellman

---

5 Lowell first met JKO at a 1962 White House state dinner with his wife, author Elizabeth Hardwick. Prone to manic episodes, Lowell later became convinced that Jackie wanted to marry him and sent her long, rambling letters. This was quickly discouraged by the Secret Service.

The Feminine Mystique, Betty Friedan

Anna Karenina, Leo Tolstoy

The Age of Napoleon, Katell Le Bourhis

A Woman's Life in the Court of the Sun King, Duchess d'Charlotte-Elisabeth Orléans (gift from Michael of Greece)

The Roosevelt Family of Sagamore Hill, inscribed by Joseph P. Lash

Preface à Sumer, André Malraux

ON MARILYN'S BOOKSHELF

Contrary to popular perception, MM was a wide and varied reader and had more than four hundred books in her personal library, covering art history, psychology, philosophy, literature, religion, poetry and gardening. In 1945, she had a library card from the Westwood Public Library and opened her first charge account at a bookstore in 1946. In 1951, Marilyn even took a night course at UCLA, "Backgrounds in Literature."

After she became famous, she had friendships with literary greats such as T. S. Eliot (they had a long-running correspondence), Carl Sandburg and Marianne Moore.

Some of her favorite authors included Fyodor Dostoyevsky, J. D. Salinger, George Bernard Shaw, Walt Whitman, Thomas Wolfe, John Keats. After her acting teacher Michael Chekhov died, she bought his library on an installment plan when she was just starting out as a contract player at Fox Studios.

Browsing among her library would make any English major's heart beat just a little faster (well, more than a little).

Among the first editions was her own copy of the beat-generation classic *On the Road* by Jack Kerouac, Ralph Ellison's *The Invisible Man* and William Styron's *Set This House on Fire*. There was also F. Scott Fitzgerald's *The Great Gatsby*, Lewis Carroll's *Alice's Adventures in Wonderland*, James Joyce's *Dubliners*, Ernest Hemingway's *The Sun Also Rises*, and *The Fall* by Albert Camus. Her library also contained her bibles and children's books, including (our personal favorite) *The Little Engine That Could*.

Other books in MM's library included:

Psychology of Everyday Life, Sigmund Freud

Life Among the Savages, Shirley Jackson

The Importance of Living, Lin Yutang

Goodnight, Sweet Prince, Gene Fowler

Greek Mythology, Edith Hamilton[6]

The Course of My Life, Rudolf Steiner

Stanislavsky Directs, Michael Gorchakov

Lust for Life, Irving Stone

To the Actor, Michael Chekhov

The Thinking Body, Mabel Elsworth Todd

The Web and the Rock, Thomas Wolfe

An Actor Prepares, Kostantin Stanislavski

---

6 Interestingly, JKO gave RFK this book after JFK died to try to help him make sense of the tragedy.

Autobiography of Lincoln Steffens

Science and Health with Key to the Scriptures, Mary
   Baker Eddy

Biography of Eleanora Duse, William Weaver

Your Key to Happiness, Harold Sherman

J+M GALS—LIBRARY OF TODAY

The Jackie of today is literary in the old-fashioned sense: She knows her Shakespeare, Yeats, F. Scott Fitzgerald, and Edna St. Vincent Millay (she knows, too, that Edmund Wilson was Fitzgerald's literary champion since their days at Princeton and that "Bunny" Wilson was madly in love with Edna Millay for years). Today, she would probably prefer real books to Kindle, although she sees the use of an e-reader when traveling abroad.

The Marilyn of today is also a great reader, but she wears her bookishness less obviously than the Jackie. Instead, beaux and admirers are surprised when they visit her home and see the piles of hardcover books (mostly heavy tomes on art, psychology and biography) strewn about. Sometimes, when she is having her picture taken, she will be reading a book, and this will surprise people, too.

HEREWITH, THE ABRIDGED (AND HIGHLY ARBITRARY) J+M LIBRARY OF TODAY . . .

One Special Summer—A reprinted scrapbook that Jackie and Lee made for their mother and stepfather of their 1951 trip to Europe. Jackie was twenty-two and Lee was eighteen. Needless to say, they had the time of their lives: think *The Talented Mr. Ripley* without all the scary stuff.

The Prince by Niccolò Machiavelli—The JKO Gal has to learn to navigate the ways of the world somehow.

Reporting Back by Lillian Ross—On one level, JKO really wanted to live a life of adventure and write for the *New Yorker.*

History of Art by Anthony F. Janson—A doorstop; the Marilyn is working her way through it.

Anything written by Pema Chödrön—It might not help, but the JKO Gal is willing to give it a try.

The Gospel According to Coco Chanel by Karen Korbo—Of course she already knows most of this stuff by heart, but the JKO Gal would read this to gild the lily, as it were.

The Best and the Brightest by David Halberstam—One of the few books that both the Jackie Gal and the Marilyn Gal would read. Those who do not know the sins of the past are condemned to repeat them.

Pools by Kelly Klein—Since the Marilyn Gal looks so great in a bikini. Or just in a bikini bottom if it is midnight and the pool lights are off.

The Official Preppy Handbook, edited by Lisa Birnbach—The Jackie Gal will skim this to see how "right" the authors got it, and all the inside stuff she already knows. Will then put it aside and never open it again, silently blessing the gods that got her away from that life . . . and those people. Very well written.

Anything by James Salter, Joan Didion, Stephen Colbert or Evelyn Waugh—Jackie, Jackie, Jackie, although MM will drop Salter's name to test her dates.

Angela's Ashes by Frank McCourt—The MM finds comfort in a childhood worse than her own.

The March of Folly by Barbara Tuchman—The JKO on a history kick.

The Happy Summer Days by Fulco—JKO, def. A society memoir, Verdura palled around with Chanel and Doris Duke *and* is the designer of some of the most gorgeous jewelry in the world—what more does a gal want?

Life at the Marmont by Raymond Sarlot and Fred E. Basten—The MM is visualizing herself poolside, getting discovered.

My Life With The Saints by James Martin, SJ—The Catholic Church is routinely battered and, well, the JKO (no surprise) is friends with Fr. Martin.

The Odyssey translated by Robert Fagles—The MM reads this one for self-improvement, etc.

Zelda by Nancy Milford—Poor Zelda. This one makes the MM cry every time.

Extremely Loud and Incredibly Close Jonathan Safran Foer—JKO, def.

Mastering the Art of French Cooking by Julia Child, Louisette Bertholle and Simone Beck—The Jackie would have this in her kitchen, just to show off.

The Secret History by Donna Tartt—For the MM, a book *everyone* was reading one season.

Napoleon & Josephine by Evangeline Bruce—Sigh. The Jackie would move to France in an *instant*.

Sophie's Choice by William Styron (signed)—JKO met him once at a party and never recovered. . . . and have you seen his sons?

Collected Poems by Robert Penn Warren (signed)—MM met *him* at a party and instantly fell in love.

Dead Poet's Society (script)—Memorized by the Marilyn Gal. Carpe diem and all that.

The Estate of Jacqueline Kennedy Onassis, April 23–26, 1996, Sotheby's—As if she needs more inspiration, the Jackie Gal uses it for future reference.

The Marilyn will also read tons of movie books—bios of Billy Wilder, James Dean, Barbara Stanwyck, Joe Eszterhas, *You'll Never Eat Lunch in This Town Again* by Julia Phillips, *Inside "Inside"* by James Lipton, *The Last Tycoon* by F. Scott Fitzgerald, *The Kid Stays in the Picture* by Robert Evans, *Vanity Fair: The Portraits* by Graydon Carter.

Lovingkindness by Sharon Salzberg—The Marilyn, because she's *got* to start being kinder to herself and stop being such a perfectionist. (She's trying, but honestly, it's not really working.)

The Balthazar Cookbook by Keith McNally—The Jackie's. Spine has never been cracked.

J+M MIND-SET: HEAD GAMES

When the situation called for it, Jackie was very disciplined, while Marilyn was, shall we say, whimsical.

If something was bothering JKO (whether it was her husbands' infidelities, a situation she did not like, a person who was bothering her), her basic MO would be to ignore it. Or them.

When Martha Stewart got herself invited to have lunch with Jackie and a Doubleday coworker in Los Angeles in the mid-1980s, Martha (for whatever reason) was almost an hour late.

An hour late. For lunch. With Jacqueline Kennedy Onassis.

Did Jackie say anything? Did she ask why the then-largely unknown Martha Stewart was late? Did she care?

No. Instead, Jackie never could remember Martha's name when it came up after that, referring to her as "that pretty girl. . . ." And she made it clear that she could never figure out what the heck Martha did for a living, anyway—didn't people already know how to put cookies on a decent plate or flowers in a vase?

Both Jackie and Marilyn presented themselves to the world as they wanted to be seen. When she was dating, Marilyn quickly realized that men liked a "happy" girl; they didn't want to hear her troubles. So the "real" Marilyn—the public Marilyn—was a bit of a subterfuge. But this is how she decided to be.

Similarly, Jackie's strength of mind helped her to consciously create herself as she wanted to be; for example, as a woman in a loving, solid marriage to JFK. While he may have loved her in his own way (he admitted, "I'm just not a flowers and candy guy"), they never did have a middle class, monogamous,[7] "Honey, I'll be home for dinner at six," kind of relationship.

Jackie, like Marilyn, was essentially an actress. Priscilla Mc-Millan, a friend of JFK's, once said of Jackie: "I always felt from the first moment I met her that I was in the presence of a great actress." JFK was a bit of an actor himself. He portrayed himself as robust and athletic, but in reality, he was a sickly child and as an adult suffered from Addison's disease, a chronic condition characterized by the withering away of the adrenal glands.

With the Kennedys, there were always boxes within boxes, secrets within secrets, and situations some knew about but others did not. Typical of the Irish, quite a bit was never discussed.

Interestingly, both Marilyn's and Jackie's favorite movie was *Gone With the Wind*. One thinks of Scarlett O'Hara's overall head-in-the-sand mentality and her mantra: "Tomorrow is another day."

IT'S ALL IN THE HAND: JACKIE VS. MARILYN

Although Jackie and Marilyn never met, Jackie was no dummy and certainly knew that her husband was infatuated with Marilyn Monroe (like the rest of the world). As an inquiring photographer for the *Washington Times-Herald* (before she even knew JFK), Jackie asked bystanders, "If you had a date with Marilyn Monroe, what would you talk about?"

But what if Jackie and Marilyn *had* met—and there is no evidence that they ever did, except in some *Weekly World News* alternative universe. Would they get along? What would their interaction be like?

To find out, we asked world-famous graphologist Arlyn Imberman to analyze Jackie's and Marilyn's handwriting.

. . . .

7 On JFK's part, anyway. There was never any marital scandal associated with JKO in this regard. Ever.

According to Imberman's assessment, "Jackie was a woman of mystery and great subtlety—a person of fortitude and discipline. Marilyn would, no doubt, be effusive and long for approval, which Jackie would delight in denying.

"Marilyn was a woman of spontaneity, anxiety and self-indulgence. Unlike Jackie (whose career was perfecting her persona), Marilyn had no insulation. They each had a separate public self, but Marilyn often blurred the lines between the two.

"Jackie's disdain would lower the room temperature, and with the movement of an eyebrow, reduce Marilyn to Jell-O.

"Marilyn believed elegance was excess; Jackie believed elegance was refusal. They were both canvases one could project one's fantasies upon."

 JACKIE'S FAVORITE MUSIC

Jackie loved all kinds of dance music and loved to dance—the twist, the cha-cha. In the 1960s, she took lessons in the frug and the watusi (ask your parents or grandparents) from society dance instructor Frank "Killer Joe" Piro. Jackie also liked Broadway musicals like *Candide* and *Camelot,* as well as anything by Leonard Bernstein.

Other favorites:

Meyer Davis Orchestra

1950s jazz

Miles Davis

Elvis Presley's "Blue Suede Shoes"

"The Girl from Ipanema"

"On a Clear Day You Can See Forever" by Alan Jay Lerner

Paul McCartney and Wings—JKO went to a concert and apparently loved it(!)

Carly Simon

In later years, taking a cue from her son John, she also liked the Rolling Stones and the Grateful Dead.

 MARILYN'S FAVORITE MUSIC

Marilyn loved music of all kinds—jazz and the blues particularly. She also, famously, personally integrated the Mocambo (a well-known Los Angeles club) in the 1950s by lobbying the owner to book Ella Fitzgerald and promising to sit at a front table every night for a week if he did so.

Frank Sinatra

Gertrude Lawrence

Gertrude Niesen

Janice Mars

Ella Fitzgerald

Charlie "Bird" Parker

J+M CHARACTER-BUILDING EXERCISE: GET OFF THE WWW ONCE IN A WHILE

Some words of advice to you, oh Jackie or Marilyn-esque Gal. Were they alive today, we think that both JKO and MM would be in the throes of a nascent (or not-so-nascent) Internet obsession because they both had somewhat addictive personalities.

We imagine that Jackie would be more of a www gal for her love of shopping (hello, giltgroupe.com!) and continuing interest in politics and world events, as well as reading books and trending somewhat toward excessive exercise habits.

Marilyn favored champers and daytime indolence; we think she would be more technology-averse. Today she would rarely read or send emails (and take pride in this) and would probably pay one of her assistants to program her iPod with her favorite music.

And then leave it in the back of a limo somewhere.

FUNNY GIRL(S)

Both Jackie and Marilyn were funny. We're not talking slapstick comedy, but funny enough that people commented on it.

(For some reason, people are always surprised when a beautiful woman is funny.)

Their humor—that most personal thing—reflected their personalities. Jackie was wry, a little bit cutting. Once, commenting to another friend about Pamela Harriman, who was part of their social set and made a point of only becoming involved with rich, powerful men who underwrote her lifestyle, Jackie described her as "a bit of a feeder fish." She also did devastating imitations of famous people after she had met them (Charles de Gaulle was apparently a favorite). In the White House, Tish Baldrige remembers, "She imitated people, heads of state, after everyone had left a White House dinner. Their accents, the way they talked. She was a cutup. Behind the closed doors, she'd dance a jig."

Marilyn was more winsome. Ambushed by reporters after she returned from Mexico, having gotten a secret-ish divorce from Arthur Miller, she said, "I am upset and I don't feel like being bothered with publicity right now," and then realizing that the reporters needed something quote-worthy, smiled and continued, "but I would love to have a plate of tacos and enchiladas—we didn't have time for food in Mexico."

Jackie scared you a bit with her humor. The head girl at school, she was that smart and unafraid and let you know it. Marilyn, with little guile, just wanted you to love her.

THE JACKIE PSYCHE: KEEP YOUR EYE ON THE PRIZE

Jackie kept her eye on the prize. Always. She was the kind of a gal who asked for a prenup and got the best attorney in town (or her former brother-in-law) to negotiate it for her, and then read the fine print. She noticed what gifts she received from her significant other on birthdays and Christmas (Valentine's Day, like Saint Patrick's Day and New Year's Eve, is for pikers). And while homemade gifts were encouraged from her nephews and nieces and her own children, the man in her life had better come up with something major in a small leather box—say, Van Cleef & Arpels or Harry Winston. Securities, land and Impressionist paintings also made good gift ideas.

For Jackie, money, and the security it brings, was paramount.

A true Leo, the Jackie Gal is a winner. This is how she was raised. This is what is expected of her and, truth be told, how she sees herself. In Jackie's case, perception is reality, and she does not suffer too many bouts of uncertainty or self-pity. In general, the Jackie thinks she is pretty terrific and is not surprised to find that the world does, too.

. . . .

THE MARILYN PSYCHE: YOU ARE DESTINED TO BE A STAR

. . . .

Marilyn was noticeably more vulnerable than Jackie (who had the essential tough-guy nature needed to thrive during life with the Kennedys). With the exception of abandoned puppies and kittens, she was practically more vulnerable than anyone.

For Marilyn, respect was more important than status, fame or money. She was more apt to take lost stragglers under her wing, fall for a sob story, loan money to her maid, give money to good causes (particularly those that helped homeless animals or orphans) and rework her will, leaving everything to her acting coach.

In her mind (regardless of her current celebrity or status), she was still the underdog. She would always be the underdog. And yet, she was a *star* with a capital *S,* and she knew it. She had beauty, talent and the desire to move beyond her humble beginnings to become her own glorious creation: *Marilyn.*

Whether an actress, accountant,[8] fashion editor or studying for the bar exam, the Marilyn Gal of today is always appearing in her own screenplay. A romantic comedy, a tragedy, a love story or somewhere in between, the Marilyn is always the star of that production called *My Life.*

As children, both the Marilyn and the Jackie Gals wanted to lead a big life, to be "someone." (Or at least create an impression while they are here.)

. . . .

8 An unlikely Marilyn-esque occupation, we admit.

J+M FIELD NOTES: ON THE COUCH WITH LES GALS

Surprising to those who know her, the Jackie Gal goes to a shrink and actually enjoys it. She is so closemouthed about pretty much everything going on in her life that her friends can't imagine her confiding in anyone about anything. But she gets a secret kick out of her 50-minute, once-a-week session—she thinks of it like being on the *Charlie Rose Show* (sort of) and tucks away interesting stories and observations to share with the doctor.

Overall, the Jackie finds the whole process (i.e., herself) pretty fascinating.

She considered asking him to sign a confidentiality agreement (if she is not famous now, she is confident she will be in the near future) but decided against it; she didn't want to offend him.

The Marilyn (not surprisingly) is an enthusiastic proponent of psychiatry, and visits to her shrink are more like performance art. She loves going. To her, it's like a date, only without the dinner and candlelight (and the whole sex thing afterward, obviously). She loves being listened to with any kind of intensity and even plans what she is going to wear in advance (see? the perfect date). She would go five times a week, for hours at a time, if she could. She loves talking and thinking about herself. With all kinds of boundary issues (sometimes troubling, gen-

erally charming), the Marilyn practically wills her psychiatrist (Jewish, male, intellectual, happily married) to fall in love with her.

He might, but nothing ever comes of it.

YOU DON'T NEED AN IVY-LEAGUE DEGREE TO SHINE

Face it: After you are out of school for a year, it is sort of loser-ish to still be name-dropping about where you got your degree—*who cares!* If you were fortunate enough to ace the SAT and get a scholarship or have parents who underwrote the operation, that's great. We are all for higher ed, but frankly, some of the coolest people we know didn't even finish college.[9]

And Marilyn? No—Marilyn is not someone who went to college. She is someone who left home as soon as she could (whether literally or metaphorically).

Never stop learning.

Don't be afraid to ask questions.

Do your research. In this age of Google and the Internet, it's easier to check a historical figure, a fact, or the correct meaning of a word without having to haul yourself to a library and pull out an actual book. So there are no excuses for "not knowing" something.

Be taken seriously. Even if you are deeply sexy (and the Marilyns of today are), you should know your stuff. Because for even the prettiest supermodel, dumb gets old fast. If you are looking for a role model, think Christy Turlington—a supermodel of the 1980s and '90s who went on to become a human rights advocate, businessperson and graduate from NYU and Columbia University.

9 Bill Gates, Steve Jobs, Jann Wenner, three-quarters of Hollywood . . .

SECRET SECRETS—THE JACKIE: THINGS YOU MIGHT NOT KNOW ABOUT HER

For such a famous person, Jackie actually loved being alone and relished her privacy. There was no entourage for her.

SECRET SECRETS—THE MARILYN: THINGS YOU MIGHT NOT KNOW ABOUT HER

In 1999, Marilyn's private library was sold in a record-breaking Sotheby's auction. The proceeds from this specific sale benefited Literacy Partners in New York City.

Jackie and Marilyn at Work: Professional Demeanor and Achievements

"What matters is what you get up on the screen—the art."

—MM

. . . .

"My name is Jacqueline Kennedy Onassis, I am an editor, and I am now working on a book."

—JKO

*R*egardless of how frothy she appeared on-screen, Marilyn was deeply intent on being an actress, a star—on having her own career and being taken seriously. As she put it, "My work is the only ground I've ever had to stand on." Unlike Jackie, she was not interested in money, per se, but the respect of her peers and the audience. "I want to be an artist and an actress with integrity. . . . I don't care about the money," she admitted. "I just want to be wonderful."

Perhaps because she was the wife of a beloved president or born on the right side of the tracks, Jackie (except for a slight dip in public opinion during her free-spending Onassis years) always had respect. Whether overseeing the restoration of the White House while first lady or working as a book editor in the mid-1970s until her death, she was as conscientious as a schoolgirl. She did not miss deadlines, and as an editor, she coddled her writers with the attention that most writers dream about.

Marilyn's one great dream was to be a movie star, to become famous, because it would put an end—once and for all—to the indignities she had suffered in her youth. Unlike Jackie, she did not marry for security (as she could have any number of times). But the possibility—that necessity of being an actress, of greatness, of being *known*—really drove her.

Both Jackie and Marilyn wanted a stable home life, and both dreamed of having children (because of gynecological problems, Marilyn was unable to bear children and suffered because of this), but both Jackie and Marilyn (on some level) also wanted to live a big life—an exciting life, too.

The Marilyn Gal of today would set her sights on what she wanted and go after it with the tenacity of someone with nothing to lose. While Jackie might be subtler in her direct dealings with power (as she could afford to be), at the end of the day, both Marilyn and Jackie would get what they wanted.

*M*arilyn needed to be a success. Even at the beginning, when she was just starting out on her first modeling shoots, she took it very, very seriously. David Conover, one of the first photographers who discovered her in 1944, said that he had never met anyone so driven.

"There was a luminous quality to her face," he recalled years later, "a fragility combined with astonishing vibrancy." He also said that he could not recall any other model so self-critical. Dissatisfied with anything less than perfection, Marilyn wanted every image of herself to be brilliant.

THE FAME GAME

"Fame will go by, and, so long, I've had you fame . . . it's something I experienced, but that's not where I live."

— MM

. . . .

"The sensational pieces will continue to appear as long as there is a market for them. One's real life is lived on another private level."

— JKO

Did either Jackie or Marilyn trust fame? Both of them, having known celebrity and its price and rewards, certainly knew the cost of it. As Marilyn observed, fame at the level she (and Jackie) experienced it almost turns a person into a thing. "It stirs up envy, fame does. People . . . feel fame gives them some kind of privilege to walk up to you and say anything to you—and it won't hurt your feelings—like it's happening to your clothing."

If a comparison were made, Marilyn was probably more purely ambitious for her own sake. She had to be. Having come from nowhere, she needed fame far more than Jackie, if only to give herself definition as well as a sort of stand-in currency for love and acceptance. A child of Hollywood, she remade herself more thoroughly than Jackie—from a neglected little girl named Norma Jeane Baker to the sexy, platinum goddess Marilyn Monroe.

In spite of the fact that she was "the most famous woman in the world," Jackie never considered what she did as particularly important; instead, she felt that what she had was almost reflected glory (whether these were her true thoughts or merely good WASP breeding, it is hard to say). As the daughter and wife of two famous men, Jackie never really felt that she came into her own until she worked as an editor in publishing. Once, swimming on Martha's Vineyard with her friend Carly Simon, there were helicopters overhead, and Jackie looked up and said, "Look, Carly—they must know you're here!"

But putting aside her disingenuousness—this is a woman, after all, who sent her maid out to buy copies of the *New York Post* and the *National Enquirer* and savored any mention of herself[1]—Jackie used her fame for her own ends, like when she wanted to restore the White House, for example, or save Grand Central Terminal from the wrecking ball. In other words, she wanted it both ways. She wanted to control her image and be able to move freely in the world, taking photographer Ron Galella to court (and winning) when he harassed her children, donning dark sunglasses—or using wigs, fake accents and disguises—to walk around New York City unmolested. But she also wanted to be able to use her fame when it counted, from attending a press conference to save Saint Bartholomew's Church from having an office tower built over it to her campaign to preserve Grand Central Terminal.

The first victims of the paparazzi era (and god knows what Marilyn would have been subjected to today, when lesser Monroe doppelgängers like Lindsay Lohan or Paris Hilton are endlessly harassed), both Jackie and Marilyn were exceedingly aware of the public "self" they presented, and they took pains to preserve it the way they wanted to. Sporty Jackie with her brown bob and dark sunglasses, mysterious as she smiled and walked quickly away. Marilyn in a white silk dress cut deep in front, bare legged, laughing over a subway grate, her skirt billowing up, thrilled by the sexual havoc she caused.

Whether wanting to become a movie star or save a historical monument, both Jackie and Marilyn used fame to their own ends.

. . . .

1 Once, when he was a boy, JFK Junior asked his mother to buy him an ice cream cone. She said no, she did not have any money. Throwing a slight tantrum, he said, "What do you mean? You're the richest woman in the world!" So yes, even her children knew of her reputation. [BTW, the tantrum didn't work.]

When Your Name Is on the Front Door, Everything Matters—
Jackie took her duties seriously. After JFK was assassinated,
she was obsessed with the thought that America and the world
would forget her husband. She devoted herself to protecting and
promoting his legacy by building the JFK Library (originally supposed to be on the Harvard campus, it is now in Columbia Point,
overlooking Boston Harbor), and by encouraging everyone in his
administration, from heavies like National Secretary of Defense
Robert McNamara to Larry Arata, the White House upholsterer,
to submit to an oral history about their time in the White House.
Currently housed in the archives of the JFK Library, these interviews are a vital research tool used to this day.

After choosing I. M. Pei, a then-unknown architect, to design the soaring building, Jackie devoted herself to fund-raising
for the library. To everyone who donated $1,000, she sent a
personal thank-you note.

And, of course, being Jackie, she would not really be involved
in the library if she did not get involved in the aesthetics—and
she was, down to the placement of the stones and sea grass
around the building and even the recipe for the New England
clam chowder served in the restaurant. When Jackie made site
visits, workers were known to try to hide, she could voice her
opinions so strongly. But then, if you visit the JFK Library today,
the hand of JKO is everywhere—from the delicious chowder, to
the beautiful grounds and even the small flower arrangements
on each table in the café.

*P*rotect the Brand—MM was so proprietary about her own
look that when she started filming *Bus Stop,* she became convinced that lesser costar Hope Lange's (in one of her first major
roles) hair was competing with her own. The producer, director
and her makeup team tried to convince her that she, Marilyn,
was the true platinum blonde and Hope was a lesser blonde
and therefore no competition, but MM was having none of it.

The Divine Miss M (in true diva style) shut down production for three days as the fair-haired Lange was progressively dyed darker and darker until she was a more earthbound brown.

The lesson? *Nobody* messes with the blonde.

*D*on't Sell Yourself Short—In work situations, take yourself seriously. In Monroe's day, movie stars did not appear on the small screen, except for a brief appearance she made in 1953 on *The Jack Benny Show,* when she was a rising star.

As her agent said to a producer pitching a TV idea for her, "Marilyn doesn't do television. If you want to see Marilyn Monroe, look at the big screen."

Although she may have had the very polite WASP manner of making sure other people's accomplishments were mentioned ahead of her own, Jackie was not a pushover. She always took herself seriously and generally accomplished what she set out to. Jackie was single-minded in her intention to make the JFK Library a world-class library and museum near a major research center at a time when there were only four other presidential libraries, located in mostly out-of-the-way American towns.

Behind her feminine veneer, she could be relentless in seeing that her vision was fulfilled. According to Charles Daly, director of the Kennedy Library Foundation in Boston, "She was not at all above giving very direct criticism when warranted." He recalls the day she visited the library building when it was under construction. She saw an asphalt driveway where lawn and trees should have been. "She called one of I. M. Pei's guys out and pointed to the asphalt," says Daly. "She nearly ate the guy for lunch. She could be very tough."

Today, thanks to Jackie's foresight and determination, the JFK Library is a renowned presidential museum and library that allows open access to researchers and also contains Ernest Hemingway's papers.

*S*tick to Your Guns—Jackie quit her publishing job at Viking Press in 1977 when they published a book titled *Shall We*

Tell the President? A political thriller, its plotline included an attempted assassination of Ted Kennedy.

Marilyn brought 20th Century Fox to its knees when she got them to agree to her unprecedented creative demands. It is a story worth telling in full.

Marilyn Monroe first met Milton Greene in 1953 when he photographed her for *Look* magazine. When they were first introduced, she could not get over how young he was. "Why, you're just a boy," she said to him.

"And you're just a girl," he replied. Something of a boy wonder, Greene had been taking photographs since he was fourteen years old and was renowned for his fashion and celebrity images.

Rather than the usual sexy, cheesecake images that other photographers took of her, Greene produced compelling, classic images that revealed her inner beauty. Marilyn and Milton became close friends, and when she told him of her troubles with her most recent 20th Century Fox contract (her salary for *Gentlemen Prefer Blondes* amounted to $18,000, while freelancer Jane Russell was paid more than $100,000), he agreed with her that she could earn more by breaking away from Fox.

They formed a new company: Marilyn Monroe Productions.[2] He gave up his job in 1954, mortgaged his home and even allowed her to live with his family as they reassessed Monroe's career.

By 1955, Marilyn had left Hollywood and moved east, where she studied at the Actors Studio and ignored the studio's entreaties to re-sign her for such marginal terms.

Needless to say, the suits at Fox were not happy, particularly when *The Seven Year Itch* was released and was a huge hit—and they realized that Monroe was the studio's biggest asset, and in fact had generated most of its box-office income for the past two years.

The deal that Marilyn's lawyers and Milton Greene worked

. . . .

2 They would go on to produce *Bus Stop* and *The Prince and the Showgirl.*

out was groundbreaking for any actor, male or female. She received story and director approval, as well as approval of the cinematographer. Her contract also stipulated that she would appear in only top-notch productions, or "A-films." In addition, her salary was boosted to $100,000 per film *and* she was allowed to make films with independent producers and with other studios. It was a long way from the struggling contract player paid $125 per week.

Marilyn signed her fourth and final contract with 20th Century Fox on December 31, 1955.

Her contract was unprecedented, and Hollywood took notice.

No longer seen as just a bubbly blonde, Marilyn's victory over the ever-powerful studios made her a force to be reckoned with. Suddenly, everyone began taking her more seriously. In January of 1956, a year after some reporters had laughingly dubbed her "Bernhardt in a bikini," the Los Angeles *Mirror News* noted that "Marilyn Monroe, victorious in her year-long sit-down strike against 20th Century Fox, will return to the studio next month with a reported $8,000,000 deal. Veterans of the movie scene said it was one of the greatest single triumphs ever won by an actress."

> *"I feel wonderful. I'm incorporated."*
>
> —MM

MAKE SURE YOUR HEART IS IN IT

Marilyn took her work seriously, and because of this, she suffered to get it right. She was insightful enough to know she had this predilection. She admitted to Richard Merryman of *LIFE* magazine that she wasn't just punching a time clock, no matter what the studio thought best for her, "Successful, happy and on time—those are all the glib American clichés. I don't want to be late, but I usually am, much to my regret. Often,

I'm late because I'm preparing a scene, maybe preparing too much sometimes. But I've always felt that even in the slightest scene the people ought to get their money's worth. And this is an obligation of mine, to give them the best. When they go to see me and look up at the screen, they don't know I was late. And by that time, the studio has forgotten all about it and is making money."

So if Marilyn was dissatisfied with the production or the studio's support, if she threw the script on the ground in disgust or showed up on set hours late (if at all) and kept the leading man, and the director, and the set dressers, and the cameramen all waiting . . . it is not because she was thoughtless (she was not) but because she was almost too thoughtful. It meant too much to her. She wanted to do a good—no, a great—job. She wasn't phoning it in. It is *her* image, her face up there.

And that scared the heck out of her.

Whether it's writing a blog or learning her lines for acting class (or that big marketing presentation on Monday), the Marilyn of today cares.

As Marilyn Monroe said, "I used to think as I looked out on the Hollywood night, 'There must be thousands of girls sitting alone like me, dreaming of becoming a movie star.' But I'm not going to worry about them. I'm dreaming the hardest."

JACQUELINE KENNEDY ONASSIS, EDITOR

> "Lady, you work and you don't have to? I think that's great!"
> —NEW YORK CITY CAB DRIVER TO JKO

Although Jackie is most publicly known as the first lady of the United States or by her marriages to JFK and Aristotle Onassis, in reality, she spent the longest—and least publicized—part of her life as a book editor in New York City. For close

to twenty years, from 1975 through 1994, Jackie worked as an editor, first at Viking and then (from 1978 to 1994) at Doubleday.

Going back to work at the age of forty-six must have been daunting but ultimately satisfying for Jackie. For the first time since her school days and early work as a newspaper photographer in Washington, D.C., before her marriage, Jackie was not in anyone else's shadow. And although she was expected to use her renown to persuade other celebrities to write their autobiographies (some did, some didn't), she was also able to leave her public self at the door and be judged for her own abilities.

Having spent so many years in the public eye and never really wanting to be there, this must have come as a relief. As she admitted, "One of the things I like about publishing is that you don't promote the editor—you promote the book and author." To that end, she worked closely with proofreaders, designers and marketers. She even wrote personal notes to booksellers to help promote her titles.

No surprise to those who knew her, Jackie was a collegial coworker. She made coffee, went on company picnics, sat on the stairwell during fire drills and was accessible to everyone within the company. She created her own family within Doubleday, sending her assistant, Scott Moyers, to her doctor when he wasn't feeling well and scolding him for coming to work with wet hair and not wearing a hat in the winter—even getting him Theraflu and leaving it on his desk when he was sick.

But still, no matter how she tried to be just one of the gang (and she was, most of the time, bringing sliced-up carrots and celery wrapped in foil to snack on), let's be honest: She was still Jackie O. An editor from *Rolling Stone* was visiting her office, as the magazine was thinking of serializing one of her authors. She opened her desk drawer, and there were about a dozen pairs of dark sunglasses in it. After Jackie called a publishing friend and left a voicemail on his phone, he saved it for years and played it for all his friends. When she visited a national magazine, she was the only person who did not have to sign the receptionist's log, as people stole the page she signed on.

Jackie was a natural editor. Intellectually curious, widely read and with an impeccable eye for what worked on the printed page, she had always loved books and authors. According to a friend, JKO had "an unrelenting desire to observe new things." Now she was paid to share her interests with others.

"What I like about being an editor," she admitted, "is that it expands your knowledge and heightens your discrimination. Each book takes you down another path."

For her writers, Jackie was a dream editor. She photocopied pages of research, tracked down hard-to-find books and delivered them to her authors to help with the manuscript. She called John Loring, a friend and design director at Tiffany, late at night to see how he was holding up, knowing he was on deadline. She did meticulous line edits, knowing that the copy editors would catch any glaring mistakes, but she wanted the manuscript to be perfect. If possible, she cared about her authors' books as much as they did, and maybe more.

Ultimately, Jackie seems to have gotten as much out of working as her writers, coworkers and Doubleday got out of her. If anything, she almost seemed grateful to have been given the opportunity to use her mind and expand her horizons even further. "This is the definition of happiness," she said of being an editor, " 'complete use of one's facilities along the lines leading to excellence in a life affording them scope.' . . . We can't all reach it, but we can try to reach it to some degree."

Jackie continued working at Doubleday until the spring of 1994, just weeks before she died. "I think that people who work themselves have respect for the work of others."

JACKIE AND JACKO

Yes, Jackie knew Michael Jackson. Although the media (for some reason) never made much of it at the time.

Part of her job at Doubleday was asking celebrities who might never otherwise consider an autobiography to write one for her.

Considering that she ran away from any reporter or journalist who tried to get her thoughts down on paper, Jackie was pretty shameless—pitching Diana, Princess of Wales, her nemesis Camilla Parker Bowles, her former flame Frank Sinatra, even Oprah Winfrey.[3]

In 1984, MJ was riding high from the success of *Thriller* and agreed to write an autobiography for Doubleday. Well, he agreed to write a book specifically for Jackie Onassis, as he was a collector of celebrities himself. "Jackie was the only person in

. . . .

3 Oprah countered by asking JKO to appear on her show. She said no (of course). Slightly off topic, Oprah once said that her two dream interviews were Jackie and Princess Diana.

America who could get him on the phone," a publishing friend recalled.

The manuscript came in, and "it was pretty bland stuff," another editor recalled, "almost a press release." Jackie the editor, the woman who loved gossip, wanted more concrete information—What was it like being a child in the entertainment business? What were his struggles? Had he encountered any prejudice? She wanted to see the real-life challenges behind his success.

Another draft came back. Still, pretty dull.

Jackie knew what she had to do. Rolling up her sleeves and doing her best, "Okay, now Mom's annoyed but we're on deadline so let's get going" routine, she flew to Los Angeles (a city she disliked, as she associated it with starlets and considered it a kind of playpen for the Kennedy men of her generation) and went directly to Neverland.

After a tour of the house (we would have given anything to be a fly on the wall for that experience), Jackie sat at Michael's baronial dining room table and went over the manuscript, clarifying her points and, again, asking for him to reveal more of himself.

For some reason, Jackie was obsessed with Michael's sexuality. Driving back to her hotel, she grilled her coworker— "What do you think he's like?" "Who does he date?" She even asked the limo driver—"Do you think he likes girls?"

The book was published in 1988 and was a great success, spending weeks at number one on the *New York Times* bestseller list.

Still, there was some annoyance with Michael on Jackie's part. He had agreed to publish the book with Doubleday only if Jackie wrote a glowing and lengthy introduction. Jackie did not want to do it and felt backed into a corner by him.

Taking one for the team, Jackie wrote a very perfunctory three-paragraph intro.

When it came time for the book to go back to press for another printing and later to go into paperback (where publishers stand to make most of their money with a successful book), Michael refused to allow it on both counts, really ticking off Jackie, who did not consider him a team player. After all, she had written that silly introduction he had insisted upon.

She rarely spoke of him again.

> *"Like everyone else, I have to work my way up to an office with a window."*
>
> —JKO

QUICKTESTS
. . . .

The Marilyn Quicktest: Okay, okay, you do keep people waiting. But you're absolutely worth it. (And besides, no one has ever *not* waited for you, right?)

The Jackie Quicktest: You've never missed a deadline. Ever.

MARILYN KNEW WHO HER FRIENDS WERE

MM was very instinctive when it came to trusting people— whether directors, makeup men or photographers . . . or some guy who wanted to take her to dinner.

In 1962, Marilyn's lawyer arranged for her to have a new secretary, Cherie Redmond, to help with her business affairs. They had traveled together to Mexico to help MM buy furniture for her new house in Los Angeles and then to New York City. There must have been some sort of a personality clash in New York, because when she came back, Marilyn told her housekeeper, Eunice Murray, that Cherie was never to be allowed in her home. "She might be a good secretary . . . but she can't be one of my close friends."

Although Cherie was extremely capable of taking care of

the details of Marilyn's financial arrangements, MM did not want her getting too close. When Cherie needed Marilyn to sign checks, Marilyn would do the paperwork and have her housekeeper give Cherie any papers or checks at the gate of her home. For some reason, there was something Marilyn did not like about her.

"I don't want her advice on anything but business matters," she said. "Besides," Marilyn said, only half joking, "she drank up the last of my Dom Pérignon."

SO YOU WANT TO BE AN ACTRESS

Marilyn, even more so than Jackie, was one of a kind. Billy Wilder, who directed her in *The Seven Year Itch* and *Some Like It Hot,* said, "She had flesh which photographed like flesh. You feel you can reach out and touch it. Unique is an overworked word, but in her case it applies. There will never be another one like her, and Lord knows there have been plenty of imitations."

While most Marilyn Gals of today emulate the real MM externally (dye your hair platinum, wear red lipstick), some might actually want to *be* an actress. And although we know we can never dream of surpassing or even equaling Marilyn, here is some advice.

You need god-given

talent, and no one can give that to you. But desire is also essential. The problem today, of course, is that people want to be famous without really working for it, or they want to be famous for the sake of being famous (see most reality TV participants). According to her acting teacher Lee Strasberg, "Marilyn always dreamt of being an actress. She didn't, by the way, dream of being just a star. She dreamt of being an actress. And she had always lived somehow with that dream."

For Marilyn, the work is what mattered.

Study. Know your craft. Of course, the great thing about becoming an actor is that, like Buddhism, there are many paths to enlightenment—or Hollywood, as the case may be.

If all else fails, date a producer.

ON YOUR DAY OFF, DO SOMETHING OUT OF CHARACTER

Perhaps because they are so responsible (well, Jackie more than Marilyn, although Marilyn delivered the goods when she had to), we suggest that the Jackie and Marilyn Gals of today do something out of character once in a while.

Disappear

In this age of email, cell phones, Facebook and all-around Twitter ubiquity, it is cool to sometimes just disappear, if only for the weekend or a day. In a world where you are never untethered (and this is considered a good thing), it's not a bad idea to shut off all of your electronic devices and just think sometimes.

Flâneur

For the generally type A Jackie (with all of those demands placed on you), why not just go for a walk and do something you would not generally do for yourself?

Sit in a café.
Go for a stroll in the park.
Buy yourself a little something.
Make a dinner reservation for you and a friend.

Get yourself a manicure and a pedicure. This always
cheers people up.

For some reason, we think it would be funny for the Jackie
Gal to play "The Beatles: Rock Band" in her underwear (Hanro,
of course) or eat ice cream out of the container with a spoon.

Tell someone you love him (or her).

Expect nothing in return.

Iron your sheets yourself. Then enjoy them.

THE JACKIE GAL AS STEVEN SPIELBERG

The current-day Jackie Gal has a strong point of view
about pretty much everything. She can't help it; she just *sees*
things . . . the chair that is out of place in the living room, that
thread hanging off the hem of your blazer, the ice tray in the
freezer that needs refilling. Like, now.

And Jesus—don't even get her started on men who leave
the seat up. It is so far beyond her comprehension that she can't
even . . . (we imagine her sputtering here) . . . she can't even
deal with it. For her, this is very close to a deal breaker. She has
ended relationships over less.

Perfect Jackie career choices include movie producer, dicta-
tor and running a five-star hotel. A pure Leo, it is hard for her
to take a backseat to anyone. In spite of her cursory shyness,
she is not—has never been—anonymous. If she is in a room
with a group of people and there is a Q&A, she is going to get
her hand up and ask a question.

THE MARILYN SIREN AS QUINTESSENTIAL
ABOVE-THE-TITLE TALENT

Our Marilyn of today, on the other hand, is almost pure
emotion. An actress (even if she works as a partner in a law
firm), she feels things so intensely, it can almost seem painful
to an outsider. She reads books, certainly, studies art and music

and goes to museums to look at art. (The Marilyn observing a perfect nude sculpture as everyone observes her observing the nude sculpture is something to behold.) She has a flawless French accent that charms everyone, even as she barely speaks the language.

Almost unavoidably, the most successful Marilyn careers involve the arts: actress, painter, best-selling author, muse . . . and although she might work at her craft with great assiduity, it is not for the Marilyn to be stuck in a garret, alone all the time—after a certain point, she has to get out and see her people!

(Which she does.)

The Marilyn Gal has such an active imagination that you are not sure if some of the stories she tells you (about her childhood, her second husband) are 100 percent true, but on the other hand, you are in her company, so it almost doesn't matter.

To be the Marilyn's friend, to be her confidante (and possibly more), is a thrilling thing, something not soon forgotten. If you are with her, she shares great intimacies. Her beauty is one thing, her vulnerability is another. She weaves a web and allows you inside.

But regardless of her chosen profession, the Marilyn has whims, flights of fancy, mild obsessions—and then moves on. If you are a friend of the Marilyn, you must know this: Once she leaves you, she is gone. On to the next thing, the next experience.

The Marilyn (our Marilyn) doesn't take too many people with her. She can't afford to.

· ·

FACING THE CAMERA

· ·

No matter how easy—or hard—they make it look, being an actor has got to be terrifying. Especially if you take it seriously and are a perfectionist like MM was. Before she walked on set and faced the cameras, Marilyn would ask her makeup man to wish her luck and "save a happy thought for me."

JACKIE'S INTERPERSONAL RELATIONSHIPS

If you tell the Jackie something, if you mention a line even in passing, she remembers it forever (or at least for as long as you are in her life). If you give her a minute, she'll quote what you said back to you. Which is both impressive and annoying if you happen to be one of her siblings or married to her.

She doesn't flaunt it (well, not really), but the Jackie has an almost photographic memory. She reads something once, and it sticks in her head.

So you don't want to get in an argument with her. Not unaware of her power, she generally pulls her punches, unless she comes up against any kind of prejudice or small-mindedness—which drives her up the wall. Then the Jackie has zero compunction about giving it to someone higher up on the food chain if she thinks he or she deserves it.

MARILYN'S INTERPERSONAL RELATIONSHIPS

For her part, the Marilyn is more likely to use guile than a strictly linear thought process to win an argument. As a corollary, she has two fallback positions in response to any emotionally taxing situation: "cute" and "tragic"—as well as the less well regarded (in her mind) "flirtatious" and "sexual" (because that's just too easy for the Marilyn). In all honesty, the Marilyn knows she doesn't need to do much to get what she wants—aside from her sheer physical presence, we mean. When the going gets tough, all she has to do—really—is raise her eyebrow to get a response.

If all else fails, both the Jackie and the Marilyn know that they can burst into tears. This is especially useful if they get stopped for a speeding ticket.

DEALING WITH SUCCESS: DOES IT CHANGE THEM?

JACKIE—FOR A TIME, YES

Although Jackie was always her essential self and had a very strong core, it has to be admitted that she went a little bit off the deep end during her marriage to Onassis. Perhaps it was the freedom from America, from the Kennedys and their almost puritan expectations of her. Perhaps it was the ability to pick up the phone and get whatever she wanted at any time: a plane, her hair done, a massage, a necklace from Van Cleef, Robert Lowell over for lunch. But Jackie, it seemed, turned into Queen Jackie for a spell . . . with, perhaps, less regard for the millions of other "real" people in the world.

Once Onassis died and she returned to the rough-and-tumble workaday world of New York City, she righted herself and used her celebrity not purely for her own sybaritic enjoyment but for the good of others through her friendships, her work in historic preservation and the JFK Library.

MARILYN—NO

For better or worse, success changed the essential Marilyn very little. "I'm the same person," she once said. "It's just a new dress."

If anything, she was a bit suspicious of fame, seeing it as a burden. "I mean—they're going to take pieces out of you. I don't think they realize it—grabbing pieces out of you, and you—you want to stay intact. . . . They think they can walk up and ask you anything—I guess they think it's happening to your clothing or something." And while she enjoyed the attention of her fans, knowing it went part and parcel with being a movie star, it also frightened her at times. "The public scares me, like mobs—they scare me, but people individually, they react and you react to them. That's something you can trust."

If anything, she was aware of the cost of success and once admitted, "If I had a child, I wouldn't want a child of mine to go through what I went through. . . . Fame is fickle. It stirs up envy—'Who does she think she is—Marilyn Monroe?'"

MARILYN AS GIFT GIVER

Having grown up poor, Marilyn appreciated a small, velvet-lined box. She was not "crafty" (other than a stunning ability to put on her eye makeup herself), did not do needlepoint or scrapbooking or bake apple pies.

However, she was exceedingly generous—almost excessively so—with those closest to her. She was capable of handing over a Mikimoto pearl necklace (a gift from the emperor of Japan when she was on her honeymoon with Joe DiMaggio) on the spur of the moment to Lee Strasberg's twelve-year-old daughter, Susan, who was feeling ugly that day. Or, in her will, leaving one-quarter of her estate to her psychoanalyst, Dr. Marianne Kris, "for the furtherance of the work of such psychiatric institutions or groups as she shall elect" and the bulk of her estate to her acting coach, someone she barely knew.

Like her acting choices, Marilyn made decisions based on instinct, however she was moved.

Above all, the Marilyn Gal of today longs to be loved, of course. She wants to be remembered. (Don't we all?)

> *"I think love and work are the only things that really happen to us, and everything else doesn't really matter."*
>
> —MM

MONEY, MONEY, MONEY

Jackie and Marilyn had very idiosyncratic—and opposing—attitudes toward money.

For all of her high-toned upbringing, Jackie was a bit crafty when it came to cash in ways that MM never was.

For starters, her mother ingrained in her the absolute importance of marrying "big time money," and by that we mean it wasn't enough to have a nice upper-middle-class married life but millionaire (or billionaire) status.

There were other ways she differed from Marilyn. She bought her New York City apartment, 1040 Fifth Avenue, in 1964 for $200,000, but everyone (it seems) kicked in the cash to help her buy it. Without knowing that others were also contributing to the apartment fund, RFK, Aristotle Onassis (he and Jackie were secretly seeing each other, but it was still on the DL), and even financier André Meyer all contributed hundreds of thousands of dollars to "help" her buy the apartment.

Marilyn, who was *poor* (and we mean cook-on-a-hot-plate-in-your-little-single-room poor), never accepted money from anyone.

Jackie also haggled with tradesmen, cooks, chefs, housekeepers and secretaries who worked for her. One favorite technique was to pay men who worked on her apartment (painters, for example) by check, knowing that they would never cash it but instead keep it because it had her signature on it. She would also offer to "pay" by giving them a signed photograph of herself. Eventually, word got around, and they asked to be paid in cash.

Like many women of her social class, Jackie raised "pin money" by selling her gently worn or extra designer duds to resale shops on the Upper East Side.

Although she was devoted to the JFK Library and did an amazing job bringing it to fruition, Jackie—like most of the Kennedys—was not known to give much money to charity.

*M*arilyn, as we have seen, grew up truly poor, but having money was not her overriding concern. Instead, she wanted to develop as an actress, to be taken seriously by the creative community, and help her friends (all of which she did). In fact, although she had less money than Jackie, she was far more generous. She donated $25,000 to JFK's presidential campaign. Pre–campaign financing laws, that was a lot of money in 1960 (when $10,000 a year was a very good salary for a white professional male) and a lot of money now.

She was also generous to those she loved. It is a little-known fact that when she was married to Arthur Miller, she paid for all of his legal fees when he had to testify before the House Un-American Activities Committee (HUAC), as well as his wife's alimony and child support for his two children.

Although it never appeared that Marilyn had any real inclination toward excessive personal luxury for herself, especially given how famous she was, toward the end of her life, it was said that she "spent money like a drunken sailor."

Jackie also liked to spend money—lots and lots of it—but it was always other people's money.

LAST WILL AND TESTAMENT: THE FINAL FRONTIER

. . . .

JACKIE'S WILL

. . . .

To those who know their estate planning, Jackie's thirty-six-page last will and testament is described as "elegant." She obviously gave her final affairs a great deal of thought. She made Maurice Tempelsman, her friend and companion of some fifteen years, the executor of her estate, and she left him a Greek alabaster head of a woman. To Caroline and John, she left $250,000 apiece in cash, her Fifth Avenue apartment and other property and personal effects, and money in a trust that she inherited from her first husband.

With an estimated $200 million in wealth, Jackie, with the aid of her attorneys at the New York law firm Milbank, Tweed, Hadley & McCloy, planned wisely.

According to *Fortune* magazine, Jackie's will made smart use of estate-planning vehicles like trusts to pass money on to heirs and charities while reducing the bite from the tax man. In the beginning of her will, she made specific bequests. Valuable items with sentimental attachment for particular people were duly assigned, such as a copy of John F. Kennedy's inaugural address signed by Robert Frost to her lawyer, Alexander Forger. Personal friends, maids and the butler got cash gifts ranging from $25,000 to $250,000. Property went to those who would get the most out of it—her kids got the New York apartment, but Hammersmith Farm, the Newport, Rhode Island, property she inherited from her mother, went to her stepbrother Hugh Auchincloss Jr. She also thought ahead and not only left her maid $50,000 but also arranged to pay the taxes on it.

In writing her will, Jackie covered all the bases and had the final word in her affairs. For example, she asked her children to respect her desire to keep her papers private.

And they did.

. . . .

MARILYN'S WILL

. . . .

Compared to Jackie, Marilyn's will was far more quixotic (shall we say) and not as well thought out.

When she died in 1962 at age thirty-six, she left an estate valued at $1.6 million. In her will, Monroe bequeathed 75 percent of that estate to Lee Strasberg, her acting coach, and 25 percent to Dr. Marianne Kris, her psychoanalyst. A trust fund provided her mother, Gladys Baker Eley, with $5,000 a year. When Dr. Kris died in 1980, she passed her 25 percent on to the Anna Freud Centre, a children's psychiatric institute in London. Since Strasberg's death in 1982, his 75 percent has been administered by his widow, Anna, and her lawyer, Irving Seidman.

Marilyn asked that her personal effects be distributed to her friends, but Lee Strasberg never fulfilled her wishes.

It is interesting—if a bit tragic—that Marilyn, who had no real family, left money for the care of her mother, to her psychoanalyst and her acting coach. And, ironically for a woman who cared little for money or material possessions, her image spins off millions of dollars in royalties every year.

But in truth, Marilyn Monroe (perhaps even more than Jackie) transcends any will or legal instrument.

SECRET SECRETS — THE JACKIE:
THINGS YOU MIGHT NOT KNOW ABOUT HER

Jackie took her work very seriously. After all, her name is associated with it.

SECRET SECRETS — THE MARILYN:
THINGS YOU MIGHT NOT KNOW ABOUT HER

Marilyn loved her work and felt lucky as hell to have it. She needed it.

"I have too many fantasies to be a housewife. I guess I am a fantasy."

—MM

. . . .

"Jackie's house was such a refuge, so private, so beautifully done, simple . . . just perfectly in tune with the surroundings."

—HILLARY CLINTON

*O*n the home front, Jackie and Marilyn are complete opposites.

Growing up rootless and on the outskirts of society, in an orphanage and in foster homes, Marilyn did not have much of a sense of what constituted a happy home life. Married three times, it almost seemed as if she was playing at being a wife and always searching for a home—finding it briefly with James Dougherty, Joe DiMaggio and Arthur Miller. After her final divorce, she created her own life with her makeup man, hairdresser and secretary (as do many stars), but it seems she was always searching, and she died without heirs and direct descendants.

Jackie's family meant everything to her. She was very proud of being a Bouvier—even more so, certainly, than marrying into the rowdy Kennedy clan—and she drew great strength from the fact that she "came" from somewhere.

Whether her "crooked little brick house" on N Street in Georgetown, the White House, her place on Fifth Avenue, or her getaway on Martha's Vineyard, Jackie's home was deeply important to her. Because of the extremely public life she was forced to lead, her home was a place of great solace where she could be with her children and those she loved.

While Marilyn could truly be described as a desultory housekeeper who was an anxious dinner party hostess, Jackie was a legendary hostess who regularly planned state dinners for two hundred guests as well as birthday parties for her children. And although she was not personally doing the ironing, JKO was a great homemaker who insisted on having her sheets changed twice daily in the White House, French wine at dinner, and fresh flowers in every room.

HOME NOTES

. . . .

JACKIE LOVED TO REDECORATE

. . . .

Jackie was a fastidious housekeeper—not that she physically did the housework herself, mind you—but she knew how to get a proper nurse's corner on a bed or the best way to hand wash delicate china.

Typical of a woman of Jackie's background, she expressed her true personality in the home through decorating. She had fun decorating (and decorating, and decorating) the first home she shared with JFK at 3307 N Street in Georgetown. According to her mother, Janet Lee Auchincloss, she redid the front living room three times in the first four months they lived there. "And how wildly expensive it was to paint things and upholster things and have curtains made," her mother recalled.

While JFK generally begrudged his wife nothing, he finally grew so tired of coming home and continuously seeing his home being repainted, repapered, the furniture rearranged or covered in canvas, that he had a fit—wondering why there wasn't one damn chair to sit down on!

But still, he had a sense of humor about it. When his in-laws came to the newlyweds' for their first dinner party (an event Jackie obsessed over as if Queen Elizabeth were attending), JFK asked his mother-in-law, "Mrs. Auchincloss, do you feel we're prisoners of beige?"

Until she became successful, Marilyn had none of the beautiful homes that Jackie did. Instead, her living situations were more weigh stations than proper homes—a succession of hotels and (when she was growing up) foster homes. After she became a star, she bought a beautiful apartment on Sutton Place in New York City and a home in Hollywood.

Interestingly (like JKO), she was very particular about whom she allowed into her homes.

. . . .

MARILYN LOVED HER BED

. . . .

Like many Hollywood starlets—well, like most of us in general—Marilyn loved her sleep. (Ava Gardner, for example, once attributed her beauty to fifteen hours of sleep a night. We think she was kidding.) As for Marilyn, "I suppose I have a languid disposition," she once said. "I hate to do things in a hurried, tense atmosphere, and it is virtually impossible for me to spring out of bed in the morning."

"On Sunday, which is my one day of total leisure, I sometimes take two hours to wake up, luxuriating in every last moment of drowsiness. Depending on my activities, I sleep between five and ten hours every night. I sleep in an extra-wide single bed, and I use only one heavy down comforter over me, summer or winter. I have never been able to wear pajamas or creepy nightgowns; they disturb my sleep."

As a miscellaneous beauty tip, Marilyn slept on satin pillowcases to preserve her hairstyle.

THE J+M WAKE-UP CALL

Neither JKO nor MM was a morning person. They came to life, really, after dark—think of hanging at Bemelmans Bar at the Carlyle, nightcaps, wearing a white silk evening gown by twinkling candlelight.

After she became a star, Marilyn suffered from insomnia and, toward the end of her life, often depended on prescription drugs—sometimes mixed with champagne or vodka, the only liquor she could tolerate—to help her sleep. She used blackout drapes to block the light and would often talk on the phone for hours with friends deep into the night if she was lonely.

While Jackie was much healthier than Marilyn, sleepwise, she, too, liked to stay up late. When she was a newlywed, living with JFK in Georgetown or in the White House, she had breakfast in bed and then had her secretary come in to give her notes and go over the day. If she got up earlier than usual to have breakfast with her children, she took a nap in the afternoon.

SLEEP RX

Can't sleep? No need to resort to the old-school starlet regime of an endless supply of Seconal and vodka. Instead, follow a few simple rules.

Make sure your bedroom is cool and dark. Use blinds or drapes to block the light.

No caffeine. No heavy meals late in the day. No alcohol.

Don't exercise at night, either. Experts say it will give you a burst of energy (good) and keep you awake (bad).

Get the television out of the bedroom. Your bedroom should be used for only sex and sleeping. Some experts say that you should not read in bed, but we disagree—your bed is one of the best places to read!

On a related note, get your laptop out of the bedroom. One friend's spouse taps taps taps away at it all night—extremely unseductive. Same thing with the BlackBerry. If you must keep it near, TURN IT OFF! Otherwise that blinking light will keep you up all night, wondering what important news/ information/trivia/endless gossip you are missing.

Don't watch the evening news—too depressing—or read a scary book that will freak you out before bed.

Take a hot bath with some sea salts and a few drops of lavender oil to help you relax.

If you must take meds, try some natural sleep remedies from the health-food store, such as valerian and/or magnesium.

JKO FLOURISHED IN THE DRAWING ROOM

Although you might eventually end up in the bedroom, with her obvious intellectual strengths, the dining room or the library are equally compelling in the JKO lair. When she could, Jackie liked nothing better than lazing on the couch and reading, ignoring the phone. She also loved hosting dinner parties for friends or get-togethers prior to attending the theater or ballet.

Although Jackie knew how to give instructions to the cook, the kitchen was not her particular province. She once told an *I Love Lucy*–type story of attempting to cook a meal early in her marriage one Thursday night (cook's night off) and completely burning the roast. The kitchen was in shambles. She burst into tears, and her husband came home and wisely took her out to dinner.

Quicktest

The Marilyn Quicktest: Your home is the one place you feel safe. You could spend hours in your bedroom. And often do.

The Jackie Quicktest: Whether you live in a studio or a mansion, your home reflects your personality, and people love visiting and seeing how you live.

J+M LOUNGEWEAR

Although Marilyn couldn't bear to wear an actual nightgown to bed, she had lots of very beautiful negligee "sets," as they used to be called. Many of them were handmade and embroidered by Juel Park Lingerie in Hollywood (a shop that still exists).

Jackie preferred delicate white cotton nightgowns in Irish linen or very fine Hanro Swiss cotton.

Today's J+M Gals can wear your (current or former) boyfriend's V-neck T-shirt (white only)—either Hanes or Brooks Brothers three-pack. As with a pearl necklace, the more you wear it, the better it looks. Plus, any future beaux will wonder about its provenance.

In real life, Marilyn had the most beautiful feet imaginable and even got away with wearing those goofy marabou slippers at home. She took such good care of her feet, they were almost as graceful as her hands.

For Jackie at Home, there are moccasin slippers from L.L. Bean (on her, they actually look sort of chic). Delman ballet slippers. She had large-ish feet that she took very good care of but still was somewhat self-conscious about.[1]

The Jackie/Marilyn Gal of today will often go barefoot at home, great for her foot health and also rendering her vulnerable to those who don't know her too well (a rarely expressed sentiment for the Jackie Gal). Her pedicure (either red or the newly chic nude nail polish) will quietly intrigue male visitors, since she rarely takes her shoes off in public.

JACKIE AND MARILYN IN THE KITCHEN

Here's a little J+M secret—the fact that you are even allowing him into your home means you don't really need to cook anything. With Marilyn, especially, all she had to do was appear—she was the kind of gal who men didn't expect to slave away in the kitchen. She brought enough to the table by just showing up. So if she tried to do something—anything—culinary, they thought it was adorable.

But you know what? Having said that, here's another little-known fact: Marilyn was actually a pretty good cook. Compared to Jackie, she was actually a *very* good cook (which is not saying much).[2] Her typical fare was 1950s—meat and

. . . .

1 Prior to her marriage to JFK, her future sister-in-law, Ethel Kennedy, once made fun of her size-10 feet, calling them "clodhoppers." Not nice.
2 In later years, when JKO stayed at Mrs. Mellon's cottage in Middleburg during fox-hunting season, she discovered Lean Cuisine and raved about it.

some vegetables on the side, Mexican sometimes, nothing too exotic, something our parents might have grown up on. As a *People* magazine reporter observed, "She was a good cook. It was hard for her to go out so she cooked." She even had a twelve-piece Le Creuset pot set, which is something only real foodies would own.[3]

For a dinner party at Marilyn's, there might be scrambled eggs on toast and shrimp with cocktail sauce from a jar (ladled into a nice china bowl, obviously). Although fancy cooking is not her main forte, Marilyn is really great at presentation, in much the same way that she puts outfits together with such élan.

We have also seen her handwritten recipe book, filled with recipes from (among others) her masseure, Ralph Roberts. She loved Mexican food, and we tracked down one of her cookbooks—*Elena's Favorite Mexican and Spanish Recipes* (1950), a much-used, wire-bound paperback version. Unfortunately out of print, it can be picked up online at places like alibris.com.

FIELD NOTES: HOSTING A DINNER PARTY: JACKIE VS. MARILYN STYLE

When it comes to floating through life with the social graces, Marilyn had Jackie beat, because frankly, she didn't *care* about social graces. Marilyn knew that even in the stuffiest situations, she could rely on her sex appeal to get her out of a jam.

Compared to the doldrums of post–World War II America, Marilyn was an inventive homemaker. In the late 1950s, when she was Mrs. Arthur Miller and lived with him in Connecticut, she made homemade pasta, hung the noodles on the back of a wooden chair in the kitchen, and dried them with a blow-dryer. We have seen a photo of MM and Gina Lollobrigida "cooking dinner at home in Los Angeles." Lollobrigida looks as if she is actually checking a pot and manning the stove while MM is

. . . .

3 It was later sold at a 1999 auction for $25,000 ($800 estimate).

posed in the doorway in a beautiful black cocktail dress. (The way we always imagine her.)

Similarly, as a Marilyn Gal, if you are hosting a dinner party and the duck a l'orange is charred to a crisp, take everyone's focus off the mishap and direct it toward *you*! For starters, slip on your marabou mules, turn up the music and do the rumba (or a mock striptease if things are looking really grim) in the middle of the living room. Then crack more ice and freshen everyone's drink.

$\mathcal{N}$ow, on to the dinner party. For the Jackie Gal or the Marilyn Gal, the optimum dinner party male/female ratio is 6 to 1. Actually, we're kidding (a bit). Jackie was more of a stickler for arranging the table and would definitely have seated her guests boy, girl, boy, girl. But she would be certain to separate all the married couples, who are probably bored out of their minds with each other anyway.

Marilyn prepared for a dinner party the way she might for a date (or a job interview, or an audition—in her mind, they were all about the same thing), except on a slightly larger stage. This means the single most important thing is you, then your outfit. After that, it's the usual drill: manicure, pedicure and three days before the event, dye your hair platinum. All of it.

To prepare MM style, empty the ice trays into a bucket and refill. Put champagne on ice (you get three bottles to yourself).

Make sure the music is set. Arrange flowers in their vases a day or so earlier so the buds can open up. In the realm of housekeeping, Marilyn loved to vacuum, so you might want to do that for the heck of it, although, honestly, no man will notice if you vacuum or not.

Not surprisingly, Jackie was a perfectionist when it came to planning a dinner party. To her, it was all about details, details, details. Whether in the White House or in her private home, she planned above and beyond which course to serve first. The china: She had so many sets of china, she could have opened a shop, with everything from antique Chinese porcelain to English bone china to Belleek, given to President Kennedy when he visited Ireland in 1961, to Limoges. And then there was the Simon Pearce glassware she preferred at her home on the Vineyard, along with the more casual blue and white country Spode. The linen: She favored colorful Porthault or subtle Irish linen. Even which candles to use: dripless Cape Cod candles, generally white tapers, although red candles were used on the dining room table on Christmas morning.

If you were fortunate enough to be invited to Jackie's for a meal, you know she put more than a little thought into it.

She was equally exacting when it came to communications with the kitchen. Often she would write a note on lined yellow legal paper with items that needed improvement or had been overlooked. We have seen these communiqués, and they are genius in their randomness—"Sanka not hot enough!" "Please get the soufflé out early . . ." "Fresh orange juice—not frozen—for the children's breakfast."

If a dinner party went particularly well, she also wrote a thank-you note (again, handwritten on yellow legal paper) before she went to bed.

JACKIE'S DINNER PARTY MENU

For a buffet dinner in New York City during the winter, Jackie might serve poached salmon with green sauce, jambon persillée (a spicy ham dish), a Russian salad of grated celeriac or some other root vegetable, slices of paté, and a basket of good chewy bread.

She was also not averse to suggesting that someone in the kitchen pick up "a paper thin apple tarte from Zabar's" that would then be warmed and served with vanilla ice cream for dessert.

JACKIE'S DINNER PARTY MENU— MIDWINTER BUFFET IN NEW YORK CITY

Salade Russe

Sliced Pâté de Foie Gras

Jambon Persillée

Poached Salmon with Green Sauce

Chilled white burgundy, such as Puligny-Montrachet, or a California chardonnay, such as Kistler

GREEN SAUCE

For the sauce to work, all the ingredients should be at room temperature.

Mayonnaise

    3 egg yolks
    1 tablespoon lemon juice or wine vinegar
    Salt and white pepper
    Powdered mustard
    2½ cups olive oil (or canola oil, if you prefer)

Greens

  ½ cup minced fresh spinach
  ½ cup minced watercress leaves
  Minced parsley
  2 tablespoons minced fresh chives
  1 teaspoon minced fresh tarragon

In a warm, medium-sized bowl, beat the yolks with a wire whisk for a minute or two until they are sticky. Stir in the lemon juice or vinegar and salt, pepper and mustard to your taste, then beat just to incorporate (less than a minute).

Start adding the oil. Don't stop beating once you begin this process. Keep adding the oil bit by bit until half a cup of oil has been incorporated and the mixture is the consistency of a medium gravy. Then you can begin adding more oil, a tablespoon or two at a time.

Keep adding and beating until the sauce is the consistency you want. If it gets too thick, you can add more lemon juice or vinegar. To thicken, keep adding oil. You might not need to add the entire amount called for. Recipe will yield about 2½ cups.

Blanch the spinach, watercress, a little parsley for color, the chives and the tarragon in ¼ cup water, covered in a small pan. Simmer about 3 minutes, then press into a fine sieve briefly to drain.

Stir the minced greens into the mayonnaise. Serve with poached salmon.

MARILYN'S DINNER PARTY MENU

Marilyn's dinner party fare did not differ much from what she would eat on an average night. For a dinner party at home in Los Angeles, Marilyn would start with a simple green salad with sliced tomatoes and a vinaigrette dressing. She would then have a male guest (like her makeup artist, Allan "Whitey" Snyder) fire up the grill and cook either steak or lamb chops, served with creamed spinach and baked potatoes. When in doubt, be like Julia Child and put an extra dab of butter—real butter, not faux-healthy oleo-substitute—on everything.

MARILYN'S DINNER PARTY MENU— TWILIGHT SUPPER IN LOS ANGELES

Simple Green Salad with Sliced Tomatoes and Vinaigrette

Lamb Chops with Creamed Spinach

Baked Potatoes

Homemade Tangerine Ice Cream

Dom Pérignon or chilled vodka on the rocks with a twist

MARILYN'S FAVORITE TANGERINE ICE CREAM

1 cup sugar
1½ cups water
Grated rind of 4 tangerines
4 cups tangerine juice
Juice of 1–2 lemons

> *Boil the sugar and water for 10 minutes. Add the grated tangerine rind to the syrup while hot. Let cool slightly, and add the tangerine juice and lemon juice. Taste for sweetness and acidity, as the tangerines vary. Chill thoroughly, strain and freeze.*

MM's HORS D'OEUVRES

For all of you aspiring Marilyns out there, her favorite hors d'oeuvres were cherry tomatoes filled with cream cheese and caviar. No matter how culinarily challenged you might be, surely you can try this at home and serve it at your next cocktail party.

A TYPICAL DINNER AT HOME

Unlike Jackie, MM was a pretty simple eater. If you've ever watched *Mad Men*, you've seen what Marilyn might have for a typical "at-home" dinner with a friend. Out in Los Angeles, it might be charcoaled steaks, baked potatoes and a salad. Ralph would have a vodka tonic, and Marilyn would have champagne with a strawberry in it.

And actually, now that we think of it, Marilyn's very American culinary tastes were quite close to JFK's, whose favorite lunch, even in the White House, was grilled cheese and Campbell's tomato soup. As an antidote to Jackie's overly Frenchified outlook, he preferred Boston clam chowder (the cook in every one of his houses was instructed to always have a fresh batch in the refrigerator, ready to be heated), chocolate ice cream for dessert and a Heineken to go with it.

Jackie always had a cook and a housekeeper,[4] or in later years, a former nanny of her children's (Marta Sgubin) who

. . . .

4 During the Onassis years, she had two round-the-clock French chefs onboard the *Christina*.

could cook, so she always had lovely, lovely meals cooked precisely to her specifications.

- -

A Simple Dinner on Martha's Vineyard

- -

When JKO was dining alone on the Vineyard, here are a few wonderful things that Marta whipped up for dinner.

Grilled Dover sole with chive sauce and lemon wedges, or veal chop without the bone.

To cook the veal, Marta would cut a pocket in it and fill it with finely chopped aromatic vegetables sautéed in butter. She then deglazed the pan with port or marsala and poured the sauce over the chop. If JKO was alone, she did not want a starch, so Marta made two vegetables (like many rich people, Madame liked her vegetables petite)—often julienned vegetables or cabbage and carrots sautéed in sesame oil or steamed broccoli and cauliflower.

And yes, this was JKO dining alone on the Vineyard.

- -

The Jackie's Sweet Tooth

- -

Today's Jackie Gal has a sweet tooth and is addicted to Fran's sea salt caramels and dark chocolate. She also picks up See's Candies when she passes through LAX. When campaigning with JFK, the real Jackie always carried a chocolate bar (in her case, Hershey's with almonds) in her pocketbook, in case they went hours between meals.

JACKIE AND MARILYN STOCK THE BAR

The first thing to remember is that neither Jackie nor Marilyn ever had to walk up to the bar and physically mix a drink herself—that was for the man hovering around, wondering how to make himself useful. Here are some bar essentials that JKO and MM would have kept around: vodka, gin, rye, whiskey, vermouth, bourbon, single-malt scotch, lots of white wine, fresh mint (for the southsides Jackie remembered from her deb years spent in Locust Valley), simple syrup, lemons and limes, club soda.

Incidentally, JKO liked to drink Perrier in small individual bottles. During parties on the Vineyard, they were kept in low wooden buckets filled with ice (one filled with Perrier, the other with Beck's beer for John and his friends), next to the buffet table.

· ·

JKO + MM — OKAY, THEY DRANK . . .

· ·

Although she occasionally drank vodka, Marilyn preferred champagne—practically daily, as it did not upset her stomach. Her favorite was Dom Pérignon.

After the German consulate general sent her a bottle of champagne, she sent him a typed note: "Dear Mr. Fuehlsdorff: Thank you for your champagne. It arrived, I drank it, and I was gayer. Thanks again. My best, Marilyn Monroe."

Jackie favored slightly more complicated drinks such as daiquiris, mojitos, and southsides, although white wine with ice—and cigarettes to help take the edge off—did in a pinch. JFK, who drank very little, nursed a scotch all night and enjoyed a daiquiri (the Kennedy family recipe was taped to the wall in the White House kitchen) or Heineken (the beer was not yet imported into the country, but his father brought it in specially from Holland). For this reason, Jackie and the rest of the Kennedys were—and still are—partial to Heinekens and daiquiris (served on ice in proper silver cups).

For the man in her life? A really good single-malt scotch (the most expensive you feel comfortable buying, or ask friends traveling in Scotland or Ireland to pick up a bottle for you). And for the nondrinkers? Perrier or Coca-Cola.

THE MARILYN CHAMPAGNE COCKTAIL

Both of these drinks are courtesy of our favorite bartender (and when we say bartender, we mean that he is a real, old-style mixologist) Dale DeGroff, James Beard winner and author of *The Craft of the Cocktail* and *The Essential Cocktail*. Jackie or Marilyn would have loved having this guy over for a party.

BIG SPENDER

Ingredients

- 1 ounce of your favorite añejo tequila
- 1 ounce Clément Liqueur Créole or Orange curaçao
- 1½ ounces blood orange juice
- Rosé champagne

Preparation

Assemble the first three ingredients in a bar glass with ice, and stir to chill. Strain into a chilled champagne flute, add champagne, and garnish with spiral of orange peel and a flamed orange zest.

 ## THE JACKIE DAIQUIRI

DAIQUIRI

Ingredients

- 1½ ounces light rum
- ¾ ounce simple syrup
- ¾ ounce fresh lime juice
- Thin lime wheel garnish

Preparation

Shake all ingredients with ice, and strain into a small cocktail glass. Float a thin wheel of fresh lime on top of the drink for garnish.

Marilyn got blue sometimes—it just came over her. It could be because it was raining, or because she saw a child crossing the street, or because it's Tuesday, or because of something she read in the newspaper—or for no reason at all.

Jackie drank when something really awful happened to her but then straightened out pretty quickly for three reasons:

1. **Incipient Alcoholism**—Jackie didn't want to end up like her nutty aunt (Big Edie) and cousin (Little Edie) Beale (every family's got 'em), who practically let their East Hampton estate, Grey Gardens, once the pride of the Bouvier family, fall down around them, causing a great public scandal. The neighborhood children called it "the witch house" for good reason. Local grocery deliveries (sardines, toilet paper, Ritz crackers, peanut butter, no real food) were left at the front door. It was beyond charming—the house was in such bad shape that documentary filmmakers wore flea collars around their ankles while shooting on the premises. Indoors.

   After her aunt's death (and yes, contrary to rumor, Jackie paid to have the roof replaced), the house was bought for millions by the celebrity media couple Ben Bradlee and his wife, Sally Quinn, taken down to the studs, and lovingly restored to its pre–personal income tax splendor. You can still smell the cat pee when it rains.[5]

2. **Vanity**—Have you seen those women in Florida who smoke and drink too much and sit out in the sun, and then they get age spots and those little lines

---

[5] A little-known fact: JKO sent a monthly check to her aunt Edith Ewing Bouvier Beale (Big Edie) and cousin Edith Bouvier Beale (Little Edie). After her death, JFK Junior continued to do so.

around their lips (that you can see even when they're not smiling)? They look like they're well over eighty (and not in a good way) when they're barely pushing forty. Jackie didn't want to end up like them.

3. **Bum, Busted**—It's very easy to fall off a horse if you've had too much too drink. Not that Jackie knew about this from experience.

· ·

THE MEDICINE CABINET

· ·

In the realm of artificial stimulants, cigarettes, white wine over ice and B_{12} shots is Jackie, while the typical 1960s "Mother's Little Helper" triple play of Seconal, vodka and sleeping pills (sadly) is Marilyn. Champagne is both Jackie (who favored Veuve Clicquot) and Marilyn (Dom Pérignon '53).

JACKIE AND MARILYN AS HOUSEGUESTS

The Marilyn as Houseguest—First of all, even having the Marilyn of today in your home for the weekend would be a coup, so it wouldn't matter if she attempted to "help out." Although she could be counted on to get on the floor and play with the children or a new puppy, she would look at the dishwasher almost as if it were a foreign object.

However, the Marilyn will dress and look stunning for dinner (even if she has zero interest in clearing the table).

The Jackie as Houseguest—The Jackie Gal is a great houseguest in that she can do extremely specific things very well—things that generally have to do with her and/or will garner her some praise. She can make a mean cappuccino, bake chocolate chip cookies that everyone raves about or an amazing three-layer cake for friends' birthdays. If called upon, she can recite poetry at the spur of the moment, give a toast or head up a team for Pictionary.

After dinner, the Jackie will sit with the men and regale them with great stories of books she just read.

A DAY IN THE LIFE OF TODAY'S JACKIE GAL VS. THE MARILYN GAL

The Jackie wakes up every day with a plan, a schedule. In fact, she wakes up every day with a plan not only for herself but for those in her circle: her children, her husband, the kid who works in the Starbucks down the street. She can't help it—she's a Leo.

Having married a powerful man (or intending to), she is more attuned to history and her place in it. Being the behind-the-scenes overseer of a presidential library, for example, makes perfect sense to her.

The Jackie wakes up with a checklist practically next to her bed. There is staff to oversee, children to attend to, dinner menus to approve.

Today's Marilyn, on the other hand, is ruled almost entirely by whim. She wakes up practically every day and thinks: *What do I want to do today?* And then she does it.

Or not.

A midnight person, the Marilyn is a firm believer in black-out drapes, sleeping potions and eye masks. She takes her sleep seriously, claims to suffer from insomnia, and a perfect day is one in which she is not expected on set (or in the office) so she can wake up around noon.

JACKIE AND MARILYN AS MATERNAL FIGURES

Although she means well, somehow, one never imagines the Marilyn of today with children—it's too much! She is far too childlike herself to consider taking on an actual child. The Marilyn is not a morning person by any stretch of the imagination, and children, well, they like to wake up and be fed and bathed and clothed and spoken to sometime before noon. (Or so we have heard.)

Plus, children cannot be sent to the store to pick up cigarettes and French shampoo when you run out.

The Marilyn is circumspect about her own upbringing. She

may have had an unhappy childhood. There might be some vague, unnamed tragedy in her past that is never discussed in her presence (but which she uses to bring pathos to the screen and take to her bed when feuding with her director). She may suffer from unnamed "women's problems" that render her unable to bear children. She compensates by being overly protective of small, fluffy dogs, and she cannot stand unkindness (or prejudice) in any of its forms.

The Jackie, on the other hand, *loves* children. She lives for children. In some ways, it is a bid to repair her own childhood—which featured an overly strict mother and a generally absent father. The Jackie sees her relationship with her own children[6] as a way to correct this.

. . . .

IF MARILYN HAD BEEN A MOTHER

. . . .

While we have no doubt that the Marilyn loves her children, their upbringing will be a bit *lax,* especially when compared with our 21st-century, helicopter-mom upbringings of today. And while we are sure that the Marilyn loves the concept of having her own progeny (much as she loves the idea of being a brunette, cooking a four-course meal, or wearing eyeglasses in public), as a maternal figure, she is not so much neglectful as distracted. There are just so many other things vying for her attention: that new script delivered from the studio, a vase

. . . .

6 And yes, she might be seen as a bit controlling by others, but nothing like her own mother.

of yellow roses on the windowsill, the Mexican bullfighter she met last weekend in Las Brisas.

Perhaps she is between roles, or trying out some new lipstick, or about to embark on her fourth marriage with The One! And there is such hope! Such optimism! Who has time—really—to think about permission slips and juice boxes?

Still, the Marilyn loves loves loves *loves* babies—and they love her, too. Babies are so cute and so photogenic—sort of like her.

Should the Marilyn decide to take the plunge of motherhood, she needs a large support staff. There is always a nanny (or two) standing offstage ready to attend to the little darling. Either that or the children, once they reach the age of reason (say, five or six), end up being the "mom." (See Judy Garland's children, Liza Minnelli and Lorna and Joey Luft.)

If you wonder what sort of a mom the Marilyn will honestly be, see how she treats her pets. None of her dogs are housebroken. They bark incessantly and sleep on the bed. If a dog causes too much trouble, it is given away to her makeup man or secretary. Among the pets, turnover is high, so it is better not to get too attached. (This causes underlying anxiety among her children because it sends the distinct message: "Shape up or you are out of here!" And they might be right.)

If Junior asks where Buddy went, the party line is: "He went to live in the country."

As a rule, the Marilyn's kids are shipped off to boarding school at an early age, say, four. The British had the right idea ("Just look what Choate did for Michael Douglas!"). If the school has a high celebrity-parent quotient and dauntingly high tuition,[7] even better.

. . . .

JACKIE AS A MOTHER TODAY

. . . .

The Jackie Mom of today is a great mother, just as—in real life—the actual JKO was.

. . . .

7 Le Rosey, for example.

The Jackie Mother is the cool mom, the one whose house all the other kids want to hang out at. (In fact, if they are having adolescent difficulties at home, they often do.)

A few minor quibbles with the JKO Mom of today—she can be strict with her kids. She does not mess around. You stand when she enters the room (old style!). You had better remember to write thank-you notes for Christmas and birthday gifts—and by that we mean on proper stationery and mailed to her, even if you are living in the same house, and oh yeah, you know she is going to be checking on the penmanship and commenting on it. She will read the note slowly, carefully, to make sure you manage the proper balance of being loving, witty and respectful (even if you are ten years old) all at the same time.

As the offspring of the JKO Mom, there is no free ride. You are expected to get good grades, dress properly for public events (Mass, memorial services, etc.), shake hands and look guests in the eye when you are introduced to them. If you gain more than four pounds, slouch, or—god forbid—don't use proper manners at the dinner table, you are going to hear about it.

But on the other hand, don't think that the JKO Mom demands any less of herself.

But most of all, as a child, you are aware of your place in the stratosphere as the offspring of a JKO Mom. ("To whom much is given, much is expected," etc.) So if you screw up—total the car, get caught in some nefarious act, end up on the front page of the *New York Post*—it is not so much the public humiliation or even possible police record that will cause you to think twice about your actions, but more strongly, "Wow—Mom is going to be ticked off when she hears about *this*," that will keep you in line.

In real life, Jackie was a great mother. She encouraged her two children, Caroline and John, to follow their own interests, but then also had high expectations of them both. She tried to shield them from the psychic weight of being the offspring of two famous people, and in particular a beloved American president. After the death of JFK, she considered being a mother her most important calling, saying, "If you bungle raising your children, I don't think whatever else you do matters very much."

According to Ted Kennedy, "Her love for Caroline and John was deep and unqualified. She reveled in their accomplishments, she hurt with their sorrows. At the mere mention of their names, Jackie's eyes would shine brighter and her smile would grow bigger."

JFK Junior loved his mother deeply and knew that she loved him. But still, he needed to blow off steam once in a while, away from the far-reaching (but very well intended) gaze of his mother.

He did this by dating supermodels—lots of them.

Or by hopping on a plane to Memphis, renting a car and heading down to the Delta where nobody knew him. There, he hung out in exceptionally divey juke joints, stayed in a crummy motel in Clarksdale, danced (he was an exceptionally cool dancer, not like some prepster from Brown), drank beer from the bottle and listened to the blues.

No one bothered him there. No one looked at him twice. Most didn't know who he was. He loved it.

While she had expectations for her children (she frowned on John's vague plans of becoming an actor and did not approve of his dating Daryl Hannah or Madonna; for her, it was law school, and then he could figure out what he wanted to do with his life), Jackie also wanted her children to be their own people. When Caroline married Edwin Schlossberg in 1986, she did not make a move to influence her choice in a wedding gown. According to Carolina Herrera, a friend who designed the gown, "Jackie did not interfere with Caroline's wedding dress—'I'm not going to get involved because Caroline is the one who will wear it. I want her to be the happiest girl in the world.'"

According to her friend Charles Whitehouse, Jackie was a great mom because "she never said anything bad about someone else. Never even suggested things in a subtle or snide way . . . she was completely unjudgmental when discussing other humans and their difficulties. It was clear when she disapproved of an action, but she sympathized with people with problems."

J+M: LES CHIENS AND OTHER PETS

> *"I like animals. If you talk to a dog or a cat it doesn't tell you to shut up."*
>
> —MM

Jackie and Marilyn both loved animals, perhaps because animals were loving and depended on their humans. Perhaps because they would never ask for an autograph or sell them out to the *National Enquirer*.

Both, incidentally, were dog people.

Jackie owned a lot of animals throughout her life. A *lot*. As a two-year-old, she owned Hootchie, a black Scottish terrier (and showed her at the East Hampton dog show). There was the beloved Danseuse, her first horse, that she brought with her to boarding school, now buried on the grounds of the Auchincloss "farm" in Newport. In the White House, there was a menagerie of animals—Charlie, a Welsh terrier; Tom Kitten, a cat; and Robin, a canary. There were two parakeets, Bluebell and Marybelle, and Caroline's pony, Macaroni. There were also ponies, Tex and Leprechaun, and hamsters, Debbie and Billie. There were lots of other dogs, among them Clipper, a German shepherd (once, asked what he ate, Jackie grinned and said, "Reporters"); Pushinka (a gift from Khrushchev), Shannon and Wolf, which were gifts from friends in Ireland. As well as the puppies of Pushinka and Charlie—Butterfly, White Tips, Blackie and Streaker.

In New York City, the pet population was cut back considerably; Shannon, the Irish spaniel, stayed on, and his son Whiskey also joined the household.

Marilyn had her own share of pets throughout her life, mostly dogs.

Tippy was a black-and-white dog given to Norma Jeane/

Marilyn by her foster father, which accompanied her to school each day. When Norma Jeane lived with the Goddard family in the 1940s, she had a pet spaniel. Marriage to Jim Dougherty brought her a pet collie named Muggsie. At the time she was signed by Columbia Pictures in 1948, Marilyn owned a pet Chihuahua. When she moved to New York City in the mid-1950s, she had a white Persian cat named Mitsou.

Marriage to Arthur Miller brought Hugo, a basset hound who lived with them at their East 57th Street apartment in New York. Once, playwright Norman Rosten and Marilyn spoon-fed straight scotch to Hugo to cheer him up. When Marilyn and Arthur split up, Arthur retained possession of Hugo. Butch was a parakeet owned by the Millers who also lived at the 57th Street apartment.

Ebony was a horse that the Millers purchased for their Connecticut farm. MM only rode Ebony a few times.

Finally, there was Maf, a little white French poodle that was given to Marilyn by Frank Sinatra. Sinatra had purchased the dog from Natalie Wood's mother, and Marilyn named the dog Maf (as a joke) because of Frank Sinatra's alleged mafia connections. To spite Arthur Miller—boy, this is when you know things are not going well in a marriage—Marilyn used to let Maf sleep on an expensive white beaver coat that Miller had given her. When Marilyn returned to live in Hollywood, Maf went with her. Following her death, Maf was inherited by Frank Sinatra's secretary, Gloria Lovell.

~~MARILYN'S~~ MARIAH'S WHITE PIANO

As a young girl, Marilyn's mother, Gladys, owned a white baby grand piano. After Gladys was institutionalized, the piano was sold, and Marilyn was separated from her mother. Unlike Jackie, Marilyn (and her mother) did not have many possessions, so the piano obviously had great sentimental value for her. Once she became famous, she took over the care of her mother and hired detectives to track down the piano and buy it back for her.

It took them years to find it, but once they did, Marilyn kept it for the rest of her life (most recently in her New York City apartment on Sutton Place).

After her death, it was bought at auction in 1999 by Mariah Carey, who owns it today, for $662,000.

J+M HOUSEKEEPING TIP

Jackie and Marilyn were both pack rats—they kept everything. Jackie, perhaps more than Marilyn, was mindful of her place in history, and before she died of cancer at the age of sixty-four in 1994, sat in front of a roaring fire in her New York City apartment with her friend Nancy Tuckerman, reading personal letters she had received from friends and former lovers, then burned them one by one.

Fortunately for us, Marilyn did not have Jackie's same foresight. In 2009, almost forty years after her death, two metal filing cabinets belonging to her surfaced, containing receipts from places like JAX, the Ritz Fur Shop on West 57th Street in New York City, Bloomingdale's, letters, old checks, mash notes from T. S. Eliot.

On the plus side, both Jackie and Marilyn had historic sales of their extraneous stuff after their deaths. Jackie's took place in April 1996 and allowed a rare glimpse into her personal world. With more than one thousand lots, there was a ton of items ranging from Greek antiquities to silver "JBK"-engraved ashtrays. And all of it sold. The four-day sale raised an astonishing $34.5 million and showed the sentimental connection many people still felt for Jackie and JFK—JFK's golf clubs, for example, went for $1,160,000. A triple-strand faux-pearl necklace went for $211,500.

In October 1999, in what it billed as the "Sale of the Century," Christie's auctioned off about five hundred items that Marilyn left to Lee Strasberg, her late acting teacher, which then passed on to his wife, Anna. The sale was controversial because Marilyn intended for her personal effects to be distributed by Strasberg to her friends. Instead, they had been in storage since 1962. Many fans were offended because they believed that Marilyn's things belonged in a museum rather than sold for Strasberg's personal gain. Still, fans came out for Marilyn, and prices, while not in the Jackie stratosphere, were high. Tommy Hilfiger, Demi Moore, supermodel Linda Evangelista all bid. Massimo Ferragamo, chairman of the design company, bought a pair of red stiletto Ferragamos for $42,000. "A bargain," he declared. All told, the sale brought in $5,030,000.

SKORPIOS FOR SALE?

At the time of Jackie's marriage to Onassis in 1968, society scuttlebutt was that "she married him for the island." (And she did, in a way, to remove herself from the increasingly turbulent and violent American society at that time.)

In 2009, one wild rumor hit the real-estate world that Skorpios, Onassis's private island, was for sale for $170 million—and that Bill Gates, Madonna and Russian billionaire Roman Abramovich were interested in buying it.

While island owning is somewhat de rigueur for celebrities today—Marlon Brando, Leonardo DiCaprio and movie pirate Johnny Depp have their own islands (Depp privately refers to his as "F**k Off Island"), as do Faith Hill and Tim McGraw and even Tony Robbins—Ari started the whole "Billionaire owning an island" thing.

And you might think, okay, an island . . . big deal . . . until you go on Google Earth and see how big it is. We mean, check it out—it's an entire *island*. Skorpios even has its own Wikipedia entry (and, in 2001, a census record of two people living there, which sort of kills us). Besides Onassis's house, the island has a pink house

(Jackie's villa), tennis courts, parks, two lovely beaches, a beautiful chapel where Onassis and JKO were married and a cemetery where Onassis, his son Alexander and daughter Christina are also buried.

Athina Onassis, granddaughter of shipping magnate Aristotle, finally ended speculation by releasing a statement saying that she has no plans to sell Skorpios.

SECRET SECRETS—THE JACKIE: THINGS YOU MIGHT NOT KNOW ABOUT HER

JKO did not have a photograph of JFK publicly displayed in her New York City apartment. She kept a small funeral mass card photo of RFK in a silver frame in her bedroom.

SECRET SECRETS—THE MARILYN: THINGS YOU MIGHT NOT KNOW ABOUT HER

Marilyn's favorite photograph of herself was in a jeep, wearing a flack jacket and great smile, from when she entertained the troops in Korea. She carried it in her pocketbook wherever she was. On the back she wrote, "I like this one the best."

10 : *Diva Behavior*

"Well-behaved women rarely make history."
                                                —MM

. . . .

"I think I'm more of a private person. I really don't like to call attention to anything."
                                                —JKO

O-kay—diva behavior.

On this topic, Jackie and Marilyn could school us all and then some (unless Mariah Carey happens to be reading this). In their prime, they were each prima donnas in their own sphere—Jackie as the political/first lady/society babe and Marilyn as the world-famous superstar.

Both Jackie and Marilyn were divas, but MM, being of Hollywood, was the more extreme, *fabulous,* West Coast example. She had no compunction in leaving cast, crew and directors on film sets waiting for hours while she washed her hair three times, practiced her lines, or just sat and looked out the window.

Why? Because she could. Because. That's. What. Divas. Do.

Her costar Clark Gable suffered a heart attack just three

days after they finished filming *The Misfits* in 1960 and died eleven days later. And although he smoked three packs of unfiltered cigarettes a day his entire adult life (as well as cigars and a pipe, and drank copious amounts of whiskey) and insisted on doing his own stunts during a very arduous shoot (being dragged by a pickup truck in horrific desert heat, for example), rumor had it that his wife, Kay, put the blame squarely on Marilyn's unprofessional behavior. (In reality, Kay did not blame Marilyn. She was well aware of Gable's health issues—and invited Marilyn to the baptism of Gable's only son, John Clark Gable, born four months after his death.)

But these were the kinds of rumors that trailed Marilyn.

And although Jackie was perhaps more socially adroit than Marilyn (which manifested itself in some pretty passive-aggressive behavior when she was unhappy with a person or situation), don't kid yourself—she was equally adept at starring in her own diva-esque scenarios.

Although she did many good, even admirable, things while first lady, if she wasn't in the mood or didn't see the point, Jackie could—in true Leo style—just as easily become The First Lady Who Wouldn't.

She feigned illness and left congressional wives cooling their heels while she went horseback riding in the Virginia country-side because she could not be bothered with *yet another* boring White House tea. Or she might say that she was "indisposed" and then be photographed shopping and attending the ballet in New York City.

In one instance, there was a White House reception for Dean Rusk, and word got around that Mrs. Kennedy would not be attending, as she was not feeling well. When one European ambassador shook hands with the president, he conveyed his regrets that the first lady was "under the weather," and he wished for her speedy recovery.

When the president was out of earshot, the ambassador's socially alert wife asked her husband, "How is it, if Mrs. Kennedy is 'under the weather,' that I heard on the radio just one hour ago that she is in New York being fitted for a new gown by Oleg Cassini?"

The Kennedys were noted tightwads, and JFK hated it when anyone sulked or spent too much money. In 1961, Jackie reportedly spent more than $110,000 on "incidentals" (which was more than the president's salary of $100,000[1]). During the campaign, a reporter got a hold of the story that Mrs. Kennedy was spending a ton of money to look so good. She said, famously, in response, "A newspaper reported that I spent $30,000 a year buying Paris clothes and that women hate me for it. I couldn't spend that much unless I wore sable underwear."

But guess what? She *was* (spending that much on her wardrobe, we mean—we don't know about the wearing-sable-underwear thing). The beauty is that Joseph P. Kennedy—always able to spot a possible political liability a mile away—was actually picking up the tab. And what a tab it was. At a time when a very good upper-middle-class salary for a man—say an Ivy-educated lawyer or Wall Street banker—was $11,000 a year, Jackie was spending some serious coin to look so good. And further, to put the whole *how much did Jackie spend?* question in concrete terms, her secretary, Mary Gallagher, who worked full time, plus nights and weekends, was paid $4,800 a year (with the Kennedys bitching the whole way about having to pay that much).

But Jackie thought nothing of spending $3,000 on a single Givenchy blouse, hand embroidered, French couture, the whole nine yards. (And a very good copy of one of Hubert's blouses could be had at the New York City department store Russek's for $10.95.)

During the high-octane Onassis years, Jackie thought nothing of emptying out the entire first-class cabin of Olympic Airlines when she was traveling on it. Or sending a plane back to New York to pick up a forgotten antique footstool. This was,

---

1 Kennedy donated his salary to the Boy Scouts and Girl Scouts of America.

of course, decades before one worried about a carbon foot-print—or even knew what one was.

WHY THEY GOT AWAY WITH IT

Looking to our world, the Jackie and Marilyn Gals of to-day might be divas, but in varying degrees. For our money, the Marilyn Gal is always far more entertaining, far more of a risk taker and far more exciting to watch in action—since you don't know *what* is going to happen next.

But the real lesson for us today is that whether they were divas or not, both Jackie and Marilyn had the goods to back it up. They were not famous for the sake of being famous or for having been on some ersatz reality show or involved in a scandal that ended up on the front page of the *New York Post*—they were famous because they had talent, they accomplished something.

Jackie was first lady of the United States and held the country together during some of our nation's darkest days in November 1963, then went on to raise her children, contribute to society and lead a productive life. With energy, resilience and the ability to take the historical long view, she burnished JFK's legacy to a high gloss—without her, there would be no Camelot. Today, JFK is *the* president most Americans would like to see added to Mount Rushmore. Her work in historical preservation, starting with saving Lafayette Square when she was in the White House and continuing with Grand Central Terminal and Saint Bartholomew's Church in Manhattan in the 1980s, showed us that our own architecture was actually worth saving decades before most people had an appreciation for this kind of thing.

Marilyn was a renowned actress who held the world in her thrall—and still does to this day—every time she appears on a movie screen. (As director Billy Wilder said of her, "I don't care if it takes her ten hours to get on the set. No one can do what she does—when she arrives—it's magic.") More specifically (if we want to be hard-nosed and talk dollars and cents), she was one of the top-earning actresses of her time. In fact, after *The Seven Year Itch* was released, it earned an unexpected $8 million and was credited with keeping Fox afloat that year. Marilyn's magic still holds with the public—in 1999, she was ranked as the sixth-greatest female star of all time by the American Film Institute.

J+M FIELD NOTES: THE DIVA'S PERSONAL PRESENTATION

Although they were both fastidious in terms of personal mise-en-scène—the way they presented themselves to the world—Marilyn was a bit of a mess in private. But she tended to have people around her (housekeeper, secretary, hairdresser, dog walker, current husband or boyfriend hoping to move up to the front position) who kept things tidy. Plus, she looked so amazing when she walked out the front door that who cared if her bedroom was in shambles?

We think (for example) of the priceless bit of stagecraft after she and baseball god Joe DiMaggio announced their divorce and left the home they shared together for the last time. Clutching the arm of her attorney, surrounded by photographers and newsmen who had been camped out on her front lawn for the previous two days, Marilyn looked both dignified and distraught. Wearing a black turtleneck dress that hugged her curves and impeccable hair and makeup (while she still wore her sorrow like a mantle), she was every inch the heartbroken leading lady.

Jackie, like Marilyn, had a keen sense of her visual self, but she did not share MM's laissez-faire approach to housekeeping. In fact, she was the exact opposite. In Jackie Land, if you did something Not Our Kind Dear, like leave the top off the toothpaste (*really?*) or—god forbid—didn't put the toilet seat down, it was, to her, the same as murdering kittens.

Today, for the sake of familial peace, it is probably best to opt for separate bathrooms. The Jackie in particular hates slobs. She takes it as a personal affront to her Jackie-esque worldview.

And you know—she's probably right.

. . . .

JKO—Dealing with the Paps

. . . .

Jackie's relationship with the paparazzi was complex. On the one hand, they annoyed her, and she even took Ron Galella to court in 1972 for harassing her and her children (the court ruled that he had to stay 150 feet away from Jackie and her children).[2] On the other hand, she had a great eye and appreciated fine photography. White House photographer Cecil Stoughton became a good friend, creating several private photo books for her (that she loved) and always made sure to edit her selections so that she looked good in all of her photos.[3]

So it seems that Jackie wanted to control the press, control the situation. Although she sent her housekeeper out to buy newspapers like the *Star,* the *Enquirer* or the *New York Post* whenever she was mentioned in them, Jackie also fired a maid working for her who was being courted by a paparazzo hoping to get inside information on her.

. . . .

MM's Relationship with the Camera

. . . .

Marilyn loved the camera. Always did. Always, always, always. In fact, it could be said that the camera made Marilyn the iconic star that she became—and kept her in the celestial firmament. Even more than a movie camera, the still camera created the Marilyn that we know and love, even today.

Every photographer who was fortunate enough to work with Marilyn attested to the fact that she "came alive" for the camera. Douglas Kirkland, who shot her at the age of twenty-

. . . .

2 After JKO's death, John Junior lifted the restraining order and allowed Galella to take photos of him in public.
3 Interestingly, Ron Galella also tried to take only "good" shots of JKO.

seven for *Look* magazine, recalled that when Marilyn arrived for the session, she seemed "very white, almost luminescent—this white vision drifted in as if in slow motion into the studio. She seemed to give off a glow."

Two days later, after the shoot, Kirkland brought the contact sheets over to Marilyn's house so that she could select the images she liked and reject those not up to her standards. Marilyn selected ten photographs that she liked and cut up the ones she did not with scissors.

Kirkland was left with the impression of a woman in love with the camera who was also a consummate professional.

And the paps? Although the paparazzi were not the aggressive mob they are today, Marilyn was clearly hounded by the press. And they could, at times, be almost frighteningly intrusive, like when she tried to marry Joe DiMaggio in a quiet civil ceremony in San Francisco, or when their divorce was announced several months later. It is almost scary to see the mob surrounding her.

Still, unlike Jackie, Marilyn was always gracious and took the time to pose (when at a movie premiere, for example) and stop and speak to her fans and photographers when she could, even in her "private" time.

IN POPULAR CULTURE

Although they might not be carbon copies, gals with the mojo of JKO and MM are all around us. A few of today's more notable examples—

· ·
THE JACKIES
· ·

Amanda Burden, Tory Burch, Michelle Obama, Natalie Portman, Jennifer Garner, Kate Spade, Diane Sawyer, Marina Rust, Susan Fales-Hill, Marjorie Gubelmann, Cate Blanchett, Iman, Tina Fey, Cynthia Rowley, Anna Wintour, Amanda Brooks, Katie Holmes, Cornelia Guest, Patricia Duff, Diane Von Furstenberg (with MM overtones), Patricia Clarkson, Minnie Mortimer, Sandra Bullock, Plum Sykes, Nicole Kidman

· ·
THE MARILYNS
· ·

Scarlett Johansson, Angelina Jolie, Penelope Cruz, Jennifer Lopez, Goldie Hawn, Pink, Christina Hendricks, Kate Moss, Jessica Simpson, Naomi Campbell, Mariah Carey, Rihanna, Mary J. Blige, Megan Fox, Drew Barrymore, Kelly Ripa, Christina Aguilera

THE DIVINE MISS M: BEHIND THE CURTAIN

Still, in spite of her charms, Marilyn could be quite trying at times. It wasn't all sweetness and light. For one thing, she followed her own internal time clock in regard to pretty much everything. With the eyes of the room and sometimes (it seemed) the world upon her, she was not going to walk on that stage until she was good and ready. As she herself admitted, "I am invariably late for appointments—sometimes as much as two hours. I've tried to change my ways but the things that make me late are too strong, and too pleasing."

If you were not already in love with her (rare, you probably just hadn't met her yet) or on the verge of falling in love with her (everyone else), she could be exhausting to be with. Unlike Jackie, Marilyn had no filter. This was both exciting and scary. Although honestly? Some men like The Crazy the same way they insist on chasing models and actresses who are way out of their league. Why do some men go for this? Probably because they think crazy outside of bed equals crazy in bed (however you define that).

But fast-forward to today—why deal with a woman who is, quite frankly, a pain in the ass? It has always been our theory that if she is pretty enough, a man will put up with just about anything to be with her. *Anything.* Or maybe he likes a challenge or is going to be the one to "fix her." Of course, he won't be.

Even we know that.

> *"I've been on a calendar but never on time."*
> —MM

FRIENDSHIP WITH JKO / MM: IS IT WORTH IT?

To be honest, Jackie (somewhat a product of her generation) did not have much use for female friends until later on in life.

When she was growing up and in the White House, her sister, Lee, was her confidante. (Truman Capote, for his part, called them "the whispering sisters.") Once, when Lee's first husband, Michael Canfield, was courting her, he took the Bouvier gals on a rowboat ride in Central Park. He grew concerned as he watched them discussing what seemed to be a matter of great importance. Was there a family illness? Some great tragedy in the wings?

Later, he asked and was told, "Gloves."

Marilyn, on the other hand, truly loved and depended on the company of women. Growing up without a sister or a mother she could depend on, she surrounded herself with older, maternal figures, such as her mother's best friend, Grace McKee.

On film sets, she befriended her stand-in, Evelyn Moriarty, and the script girl. During the last weekend of her life, she invited her publicist, Pat Newcomb, to stay over in her guest room and rest because Pat was suffering from bronchitis, and Marilyn thought it might make her feel better to lie in the sun and use her pool.

In the last interview she gave to Richard Merryman of *LIFE* magazine, she showed him around her new house and said she wanted to have a small guest suite, "A place for any friends of mine who are in some kind of trouble. Maybe they'll want to live here where they won't be bothered till things are okay for them."

In later years, Jackie and Lee grew apart. Perhaps it was because Lee was an indifferent mother (when her daughter, Christina, was a teenager, she even went to live with Aunt Jackie for a spell). Perhaps it was because the balance of power shifted from the pretty Lee to the bookish Jackie, who grew up to be one of the most influential women in the world, while Lee floundered with what to "do" with herself (trying acting, writing, interior decorating and finally fashion PR for Giorgio Armani in the 1980s).

After Jackie died, she left nothing in her will to her sister ("I have made no provision in this my Will for my sister, Lee B. Radziwill, for whom I have great affection because I have already done so during my lifetime"), a telling sentiment from someone as thoughtful as Jackie. She did, however, leave $500,000 to each of Lee's two children.

On a broader note, in regard to friendship in general, Jackie and Marilyn were on different wavelengths. Jackie, perhaps because of the very public tragedy she had to endure with the assassination of JFK, was very adept at ending close relationships and moving on. Maybe too adept. Perhaps this was how she kept her sanity. If she felt that you had "dissed" her in some way—whether you were a former best friend of JFK's[4] or a Bouvier family member[5]—you were out.

Marilyn, on the other hand—once you were in her life, you were in it for keeps. As she put it, "I've never dropped anyone I believed in." After her divorce from Joe DiMaggio, she remained close with his son, Joe Junior, giving him advice on his love life and even buying him a car. After her divorce from Arthur Miller, she remained close with his seventy-year-old father, Isidore ("Izzy"), sending him airplane tickets and inviting him to visit her in California, something his own son never did. He was her escort when she sang for JFK's birthday celebration at Madison Square Garden. When he accompanied her to the after party (where she dodged the attentions of John Kenneth Galbraith and both Kennedy brothers), she was mainly concerned that he was comfortable and looked after.

FRIEND OF MARILYN'S

Seemingly more vulnerable that Jackie, Marilyn was a lovely friend. Betty Grable, who worked with her on *How to Marry a Millionaire*, remembers Marilyn's thoughtfulness. As the up-and-coming star being groomed to take Grable's place, studio photographers wanted to take Marilyn's picture in front of Grable's old dressing room (that was now hers). Marilyn refused.[6] One day during shooting, Grable had to leave early because her son was sick. Marilyn called later that night to see

4 After Ben Bradlee published an extremely loving memoir of his friendship with JFK (he was the Washington editor of *Newsweek* and became friends with JFK when they were neighbors in Georgetown in 1958), *Conversations With Kennedy*, in 1975, Jackie took offense to it and never spoke to him again.

5 Ditto for John H. Davis, Jackie's cousin who published *The Bouviers* in 1969 and exposed the reality that the Bouviers were not descended from French nobility but just regular folk. JKO never spoke to him or his mother again. He had to personally call and beg Jackie's assistant to allow his mother—her aunt Maude—to attend Jackie's funeral at Saint Ignatius Loyola in New York City (where she was a parishioner) or risk standing out on the sidewalk. Jackie's assistant relented.

6 For her part, BG was sanguine about MM taking her place in the Hollywood constellation. "Go and get yours, honey, I've had mine," she famously said.

how he was doing. Grable remembered that she was the only one from the studio to do so.

In today's world, as a friend of a Marilyn, you probably know some of the downsides—the teary 3 a.m. phone calls, the *beyond* dramatic love life, the missed airplane flights, impossible mornings, harrowing near-death experiences, endless Sturm und Drang (and that's just on a Tuesday).

But the question for you is: Is it worth it? Is *she* worth it? Absolutely. No doubt about it.

. . . .

FRIEND OF JACKIE'S

. . . .

Like Bobby Kennedy, like all the Kennedys, like the Irish for that matter, Jackie had a very black and white view of friendship: You were on the team or you were not. If she felt that you had betrayed her in some way, there was no forgiveness, no looking back, no understanding for any sort of human transgression. One mistake, and you were voted off the island—one need only remember her absolute ability to cut off employees, relatives and formerly close friends who had transgressed her zone of privacy.

Having said that, once you proved your faithfulness and that you could be trusted, Jackie was a great friend. Every August, she lent her home on Martha's Vineyard to Provi Paredes and her son, Gustavo. Provi had been her maid when she was first married to Senator Kennedy and later Jackie's personal assistant while she was in the White House, and had remained close to the Kennedy family.[7] When her sister Lee Radziwill's daughter, Christina, was not getting along with her mother, she went and lived with Jackie for several years as a teenager.

Jackie always seemed to know the right thing to say. When Robert McNamara was going through a tough time in the press, she encouraged him, saying, "Just remember what Eleanor Roosevelt said—nobody can make you feel bad about yourself unless you give them permission."

. . . .

7 Jackie also remembered her in her will, leaving her $50,000.

J+M FIELD NOTES: ADVICE TO MEN: LIVING WITH TODAY'S DIVA

Guys, at this point in the game, knowing as much as we do about the Marilyn Gal and the Jackie Gal, we are going to give you some advice. When in doubt, it is easier to fall on the sword and simply apologize for what happened.

Whatever it is.

We know! We know! We hear what you are saying—why are you always the one who has to make the first move, capitulate, come in from the rain, send flowers. We get that. And again, we're not saying it is fair—we're just saying . . . if you want to be with a Jackie or a Marilyn (and especially a Marilyn), well, let's just say that there are sacrifices you will occasionally have to make to keep the peace.

And yet we know—as you do—that it's a fine line because both the Jackie Gal and the Marilyn Gal abhor weaklings (of the male variety, especially). They just don't like woosy men— guys who own cats, wear flannel shirts, are thinner than they are, have nicer skin or hair,[8] do yoga.

We get that. They like a strong man who can also cook, play the piano, recite poetry and make them laugh. Plus, get their parking tickets taken care of.

(For her part, the Marilyn—dreamer that she is—ups the ante by envisioning a Pulitzer Prize–winning author who looks nice in khakis and a white T-shirt. And he must be taller than she is and fix her computer when it breaks down.)

So, yes—walking this emotional tightrope is a pretty tall order. But on the other hand, the payoff is that you get to have the diva in your life.

. . . .

8 If that's even possible.

. . . .

MM—DIVA-*fantabulous!*

. . . .

In case you are trying to picture what it might really be like to be part of MM's inner circle, here's one especially memorable story.

Marilyn was at her apartment in New York City, getting ready for JFK's birthday bash at Madison Square Garden. At one point, she was reclining on a white lounge chair, having her hair and makeup done. When she stood up and walked away, there was a perfect (nude) outline of Marilyn, her shoulders, back and legs running down the length of the chair. It seems that her full-body makeup had left an impression on the chair, ruining it.

Or rendering it priceless.

. . . .

HELLO/GOOD-BYE DIVA

. . . .

Sure, Marilyn and Jackie could be divas, but then—in true diva fashion—they could be *anti*-divas and exceedingly generous at the drop of a hat. It all depended on their whim at the moment.[9]

And again, in true diva style, you did not know what you might get from one moment to the next . . . like the weather, like rain falling in London, you had *no idea* what would crop up on the horizon, so you had to be prepared for any possibility.

This is what kept things exciting in Diva World.

. . . .

MARILYN COULD BE EXTREMELY THOUGHTFUL

. . . .

On her last movie, *Something's Got to Give,* Marilyn was at her most tenuous (and diva-esque). But it wasn't her fault, not really. Preproduction went well, with wardrobe and hair and makeup tests. The night before the first day of shooting, she called in sick, explaining that she had gotten a severe sinus

. . . .

9 Just like Elvis Presley, Elizabeth Taylor, Karl Lagerfeld, Steve Jobs . . .

infection after she had traveled to New York City to go over her role with her acting coach, Lee Strasberg. The studio doctor examined her and said that yes, she was sick and would be out for a month.

A *month*? The studio and the producer must have had heart attacks when they heard this . . . a leading lady off the set of a major motion picture (that was supposed to refill the coffers after Liz Taylor and Richard Burton's *Cleopatra* debacle filming on the other side of the world) was not good.[10]

In spite of this, the studio and George Cukor, the director, decided to begin production and shoot around her. Which they did for the next month as MM recovered, stopping by the set only occasionally.

An additional wrinkle was added to the timeline of *Something's Got to Give* when Marilyn was invited to sing at President Kennedy's Madison Square Garden birthday party, an event she had gotten permission from the studio to attend well before the picture began production. Given her late start, no one expected her to take a week off to go to New York City to sing for the president.

But she did.

So by the time she returned to the set, they were behind schedule, rewriting parts of the script almost daily—something Marilyn hated, as it made it difficult for her to learn her lines to her satisfaction, and Marilyn was not getting along with Cukor (who was supposedly a very "female friendly" director—for what that was worth). Given this chaos, the studio was also threatening (in the press) to shut down the picture, claiming that Marilyn's tardiness and decision to fly to New York City to sing for the president was the reason (although we know now, of course, that the studio was aware of all of it and perhaps just looking for an excuse to pull the plug on an ill-fated movie).

All of this made Marilyn very unsettled, feeling that neither

. . . .

10 BTW, Cleopatra (with a budget of $44,000,000—$307,000,000 in today's dollars) would eventually cause Fox to have to sell off most of its back lot to real-estate developers.

the studio nor the director was in her corner. As she put it, "An actress is not a machine, but they treat you like a machine. A money machine." She fought back with one of the tools in her arsenal: showing up later and later on set, hiding out in her dressing room, flubbing her lines and requiring take after take after take. Which exhausted the crew, the cameramen, her director and even the other actors.

Finally, late one night, her friend Larry Schiller, the photographer on set, asked her, "Marilyn, when is this going to end?"

"What are you worried about?" Marilyn wondered.

"I'd like to get home," he said. "I've got a new 7-month-old little girl."

"I didn't know you were married . . ."

"I've been bar mitzvahed too," Schiller said. "What else do you want to know about me?"

Marilyn laughed, and they sat on the steps of her trailer and talked. Schiller told Marilyn of his recent success as a photographer, how an assignment from *Playboy* allowed him to buy a little house for his family with a backyard and a swimming pool. "Look what tits and ass can do for you. Now I got a house with a backyard and a swimming pool."

"So do I," said Marilyn with a quiet little giggle.

Much later that night, Schiller drove home to find his wife up, waiting. What was going on, he wondered. His wife, Judi, said that someone had come to the door and woken her. It was a deliveryman with two dozen roses and a note from Marilyn Monroe: "Sorry for keeping him so late," she had written.

After that, Marilyn and Schiller were even better friends. He no longer had to knock upon entering her dressing room; if the door was ajar, he just went in. The next day, he brought a single rose to the set and presented it to Marilyn.

She laughed and put it between her teeth.

Similarly, John Loring, former design director of Tiffany (and one of Jackie's authors when she was at Doubleday) has a story.

John had a friend, a young African American woman, who was having difficulty getting past a conservative co-op board to buy a Manhattan apartment. John called up Jackie and explained the situation.

"Say no more," Jackie said, "I'll have a letter to you this afternoon."

In half an hour, a letter was delivered to John, and the young woman got into the apartment building.

During her publishing days, Jackie was also known to work behind coworkers' backs to promote their careers—sending a letter of recommendation for a particular job that had opened up, sharing the praise among everyone who had worked on her books.

When these public prima donnas were privately (and often anonymously) generous, their actions had one thing in common: They were always for the "little guy" versus the powerful.

DIVA TAKEAWAY: "THE JOY SHE GIVES"

In trying to understand the diva, what you have to realize is that she is not of this world. The diva creates her own world.

Charming, conniving, beautiful, tempestuous, with compelling inner energy, she holds all the cards that matter. She is the linchpin, the star, the sun around which every other planet revolves. (And what is it that even JFK, no slouch in the charisma department himself, once said? "I am the man who accompanied Jacqueline Kennedy to Paris—and I have enjoyed it.")

It is not that she doesn't care. She does. And she wants to be kind, to be thoughtful, to be that eternal, tiresome bane of women everywhere—*nice*.

But you know what? She isn't.

Her talent is too great. Her hunger, her desire, the attention she receives just walking down the street—all of it is too compelling.

By her own presence, Jackie showed us another way to live our lives, whether we are famous or not . . . both public and private, protecting her family and herself, yet using her celebrity for her own ends, her own good.

While Marilyn—Marilyn (like Coca-Cola and the Ford car) was America. When she went to entertain the troops during the Korean War, she stood on a makeshift wooden stage with only a piano to accompany her, wearing a thin dress and heels, bare legged in the bitter cold as 17,000 marines cheered. She smiled, she glowed, she waved. She reminded them of just what the hell they were fighting for. Her sexuality was both innocent and carnal, childlike and knowing.

She offered us her vulnerability and her beauty, giving the impression, always, that she was in need of protection—even though she rose to the top of one of the toughest professions in the world.

While the Jackie and the Marilyn might occasionally drive you to drink, you can be sure that sitting on the couch enjoying some Dom Pérignon in their company will, at the very least, be memorable.

They do one thing for certain: They hold our attention.

SECRET SECRETS — THE JACKIE: THINGS YOU MIGHT NOT KNOW ABOUT HER

Jackie never felt sorry for herself. "If you get out into the world, and move around a little bit, you begin to see that there are people who have been through much worse things than I have."

SECRET SECRETS — THE MARILYN: THINGS YOU MIGHT NOT KNOW ABOUT HER

Here's MM, speaking like a true diva (who, like all true divas, knows her worth): "If you can't handle me at my worst, then you sure as hell don't deserve me at my best."

"I think my biggest achievement is that after going through a rather difficult time, I consider myself comparatively sane."

—JKO

. . . .

"If you want the girl next door, you should go next door."

—MM

JACKIE AND MARILYN HAD COURAGE

*P*erhaps the most admirable thing about Jackie and Marilyn, knowing their lives as we do now—beyond the first blush of their obvious beauty, style or fame—is their courage. Each in her own way had a great deal to overcome (and yes, by any measure, Marilyn's internal emotional challenges were far more difficult than Jackie's). And each rose to meet those challenges.

If nothing else, Jackie and Marilyn persevered in spite of what lay in front of them on the road ahead. Marilyn overcame a bleak childhood to become one of the most famous actresses in the world. And beyond that, she moved past her status as a Hollywood pinup girl to be taken seriously as a "real" actress. As one of the youngest first ladies of the 20th century, Jackie revitalized the White House and added a cultural sheen to America. She held this country together in the grim days following her husband's assassination, and then went on to not only raise her children successfully but also to find a measure of peace and personal satisfaction as a book editor in New York City.

Overcoming heartbreak, grief, uncertainty, discouragement and occasional loneliness, Jackie and Marilyn rose above their circumstances and what society expected of them.

And they did it with no small measure of courage, style and élan, which we could certainly use more of today.

As Marilyn said (describing Chérie, her character in *Bus Stop,* though she might have been describing herself): "She was a girl who knew how to be happy even when she was sad. And that's important, you know."

Absolutely.

THE POWER OF FEMININITY

Jackie and Marilyn were deeply, inherently feminine; they knew the power of being a woman and were unafraid to use it. Marilyn's entire career, in fact, rested on her ability to project the feminine ideal.[1] However, like the powerful men surrounding them, Jackie and Marilyn were intelligent, savvy and ambitious; they knew how to navigate the politics of the workplace and how to persevere in attaining their goals.

Were they feminists?

Although the word barely existed in their adulthood (and MM died before the women's

. . . .
1 As does her posthumous career, for that matter.

movement blossomed in the late 1960s), Marilyn fought to be taken seriously in Hollywood, pushing for both creative and financial independence from the studios. And, famously, she won, becoming one of the first actors to put a chink in the studio system. Jackie, for her part, was a friend of Gloria Steinem's and donated money in 1972 to help found *Ms. Magazine*.

But they were also, in many ways, traditional. They both longed for marriage and a family, children even, and wanted to create a warm, private, comfortable home for themselves and those they loved. And they saw this as a woman's role.

Ultimately, Jackie and Marilyn can, in many ways, serve as role models for us today, because they did not compromise when it came to their goals and their dreams, and they did it by being women, not by trying to act like men.

ALWAYS DRINK THE WINE

As Jackie and Marilyn's mutual friend Frank Sinatra so famously put it, "I will drink the wine." And Jackie and Marilyn did, living their lives to the fullest. We have almost reached the end of our time together, so whether you have decided you are a Jackie or a Marilyn (or more likely, a combination of the two), we have one final piece of advice: Live a big life. In other words, roll the dice. Leave a trail. Be memorable.

If you're not sure whether to write that encouraging letter to a friend, write it and send it.

Laugh out loud. And if you can make someone else laugh, even better. That's a rare gift—don't take it for granted.

Look up and smile, just for the heck of it. You never know, you might be encouraging someone else to keep going.

Don't keep your heart in trust. Tell him you love him. Whether you hear it in return is almost beside the point.

And if you can give a child some confidence, that's always a good thing. He or she just might remember that moment (and you) longer than you can imagine.

Stay up and watch the sun rise every once in a while. And if you happen to find yourself on the deck of a boat moored in Vineyard Haven in August, even better.

When in doubt, order the champagne. And wear your highest heels—you never know.

You only go around the track once, but with some self-awareness and the right attitude, we guarantee: It will be more than enough.

MM CONNECTS WITH PEOPLE. STILL.

"It's all make believe, isn't it?"

—MM

While Jackie is respected in many circles and might even remind a certain stratum of American society of their mothers, she does not have the cultural resonance (along with James Dean, Audrey Hepburn, or Elvis Presley) of Marilyn. For some reason, Marilyn, far more than Jackie (with the bulwark of the Kennedys and her husband's presidency, her self-sufficiency and her Vassar education behind her), captures our imagination.

We think we could have saved her, been her friend, *understood* her—and thereby protected her.

There is something in Marilyn (her vulnerability? her beauty? her tragic Hollywood story?) that causes people to connect with her on a deeply personal level even today. Even though she died in 1962 (close to fifty years ago) at the age of thirty-six, fans travel from around the world to make a pilgrimage to her gravesite. More psychics claim to contact her from beyond the grave than almost any other celebrity. Elton John wrote "Candle in the Wind," a haunting song about his boyhood crush on her and how he would have liked to have known her, but he was just a kid. . . .

As a celebrity, her spirit is so present in the current American media mix that it is almost as if she never left.

JACKIE AND MARILYN: THEIR LEGACY IN CELEBRITY WORLD TODAY

Jackie and Marilyn never met, but they are connected in Celebrity World (think of it as "six degrees of separation" but without the Kevin Bacon factor). They were both involved with JFK, Marlon Brando and Frank Sinatra. Before his marriage, Jackie's son, John (much to his mother's chagrin), dated Madonna, who has a full-blown Marilyn obsession.[2] In fact, with her too-toned body and deal-making prowess, she might be considered Marilyn without the vulnerability factor (Marilyn 2.0).

The Jackie/Marilyn connection came full circle when, in a totally metacelebrity media conflagration (or just a way to sell more magazines), JFK Junior put Drew Barrymore on the September 1996 issue of *George* maga-

2 See the "Material Girl" music video, also *True Blue* and other album covers.

zine, done up as Marilyn Monroe, with the headline "Happy Birthday Mr. President."[3]

And the Michael Jackie-Marilyn-Madonna connection continued when Michael Jackson and Madonna attended the 1991 Oscars. Walking into the after party at Spago, Madonna channeled the full-blown "Diamonds Are a Girl's Best Friend" Marilyn, with platinum hair, 20 million dollars worth of borrowed Harry Winston gems and a white satin evening dress cut on the bias, while MJ wore a white dinner jacket, his own massive diamond brooch and white gloves.

One cannot help but wonder: What would Jackie and Marilyn have said?

THE TAKEAWAY

Now that you've read the book, here is the abridged version of the J+M ethos . . .

Lose the ego.

Take the high road.

When in doubt, wear lipstick.

If someone calls your name when you are out walking, turn and smile—it could be Ron Galella. And possibly posterity.

WHAT NEXT

We've given you the ground rules. Now it's up to you to take your utterly fabulous Jackie or Marilyn self out into the world and see how *you* can shake things up.

. . . .

3 One can only imagine how this would have gone over had his mother been alive.

"I've had a great run."

—JKO

SECRET SECRETS—THE JACKIE:
THINGS YOU MIGHT NOT KNOW ABOUT HER

It is said (among historians) that JKO kept a diary. And it still exists.

SECRET SECRETS—THE MARILYN:
THINGS YOU MIGHT NOT KNOW ABOUT HER

Marilyn collected poetry. After her death, the following snippet of Yeats (written in her own hand) was found among her papers: "That only God, my dear, / Could love you for yourself alone / And not your yellow hair."

Although Yeats's love poem was to Maud Gonne, he might have been speaking of MM.

*C*an *anyone* be like Jackie or Marilyn?

Absolutely! All it takes is vision and determination (much like Jackie and Marilyn had themselves).

On second thought, it helps to be female and, barring that, "creative."

*M*y mother is making me insane! What can I do?

Jackie and Marilyn both had fraught relationships with their mothers—Marilyn because her mother was mentally unstable and had to be institutionalized; Jackie because her mother was an Irish Catholic passing for French in a WASP world (when this mattered), with insanely high standards for both of her daughters, a very sharp tongue, no compunctions about making her views known and overall wasn't very nice to Jackie.

However, both Jackie and Marilyn chose to take the high road in regard to their mothers. Marilyn supported her mother and made sure her care continued after her death by writing it in her will. (In fact, Marilyn's mother outlived her daughter, never knowing how famous her daughter was when she died in 1984.)

Jackie also made sure that her mother was well cared for, setting up a trust fund for her and making sure that she had household staff, nurses and the best medical treatment available. In her inimitable style, JKO "overlooked" her mother's earlier treatment of her. And Mrs. Auchincloss, in her own style, always spoke very highly of Jackie to others—but never to her directly.

I don't have a perfect figure. Can I still be like Jackie or Marilyn?

Please—neither did Jackie! Not to be impolite, but go back and read chapter four—and then get back to us.

I have a date with this guy I really like. Advice?

Heels, always. And lipstick and mascara. Lower your voice. Don't talk too much. Make him come to you.

I would like to encourage my seven-year-old daughter to be like Jackie and Marilyn. What should I give her?

Confidence. A sense of history. A library card.

*W*hat would Jackie and Marilyn think about social networking—Facebook? Twitter? Email?

Email, yes. BlackBerry, def (but they would not be wed to it). Marilyn would repeatedly lose her BB, thereby giving obsessed fans even more reason to track her down.

Facebook and Twitter? Jackie—no, TMI! Marilyn would have her publicist or one of her fans take care of this for her.

Both Jackie and Marilyn would have shopped extensively online. Late at night when she couldn't sleep, Marilyn would probably respond to her fans' blogs and comments. The mean stuff would hurt her feelings, though.

*H*ow can we continue this conversation?

Online, of course. www.jackieormarilyn.com or www.pamelakeogh.com

Acknowledgments

$\mathcal{I}$ would like to thank my editor, Lauren Marino, who saw this book before I did. I would also like to particularly acknowledge associate editor Jessica Sindler and thank her for her creative and much needed (*much* needed) editorial guidance. I think she has a great future ahead of her as the Max Perkins of her generation.

Enormous kudos to my agents, who are such a great team because they combine both Jackie and Marilyn Style in their own inimitable way—Linda Chester (a Jackie) and Alexandra Machinist (a definite Marilyn).

Thanks, too, to Gary Jaffe (a Cary Grant, but that's another book) of LCA for keeping the ship afloat.

I would like to thank all the people I interviewed and who were of assistance during the research and writing of this book— Carl Sferrazza Anthony, Hélène Arpels, Rebecca Apsan, Yusha Auchincloss, Peter Bacanovic, Letitia Baldrige, Jeffrey Banks, Deepak Chopra, Darac, James de Givenchy, C. Z. Guest, John H. Davis, Dale DeGroff, David Fairchild, Ron Galella, Renée and Suzette Guercia, Steven Haft, Alexander Haas, Victoria Haas, William A. Henry, III, Arlyn Imberman, Lorrie Ivas, Kevin Lee, John Loring, James Martin, S. J., Beth Mendelson, Joseph Montebello,

Pamela Needham, Caroline Sharp, Stacey Smoker, Dr. Amy Weschler, James T. Curtis, Bob Willoughby, Susan Zummo.

I would also like to give a special shout out to Fitzwilliam Anderson, who loves to read and is deeply entertained by, and immersed in, modern American culture.

Jacqueline Onassis and Marilyn Monroe are two of the most well documented women of our time. I would like to recognize the journalists and biographers who came before me—Christopher Anderson, Letitia Baldrige, George Barris, Ben Bradlee, Jim Bishop, Oleg Cassini, Marie Clayton, Fleur Cowles, Rita Dallas, Nigel Dempster, Mike Evans, Paul B. Fay, Jr., Kim France and Andrea Linett, Mary Barelli Gallagher, Karen Karbo, Sam Kaschner, Barbara Leaming, Evelyn Lincoln, Lynne McTaggart, Arthur Miller, Jan Pottker, Mini Rhea with Frances Spatz Leighton, Cynthia Rowley and Ilene Rosenzweig, Raymond Sarlot and Fred E. Basten, Lawrence Schiller, Maud Shaw, Marta Sgubin, Fred Sparks, Donald Spoto, Gloria Steinem, Laren Stover, Anthony Summers.

One of my favorite parts of writing is the research. In addition to all the people I interviewed, I would like to thank Kathryn Felde and Mark Ekman at the Paley Center for Media in New York City—an amazing place to do research—as well as the New York Society Library (another gem). And 71 Irving—the best coffee in the city. Additional research was done at the JFK Library, particularly the oral histories, as well as the AMPAS library in Los Angeles.

At Gotham, I would like to thank publisher Bill Shinker, who leads the crew with a personal élan and vision that Jackie and Marilyn would admire. Lisa Johnson and Anne Kosmoski did great work getting this book out into the world. And tremendous gratitude to the most talented illustrator, Meg Hess, who brought our Jackie and Marilyn-esque Gals to life.

Finally, I would like to thank my friends who were with me when I wrote this book—the pizza, dark chocolate, occasional Heineken, flowers, late-night phone calls, encouragement and moral support were all greatly appreciated.

Pamela Keogh is the author of the internationally best-selling illustrated biographies *Audrey Style, Jackie Style,* and *Elvis Presley: The Man, The Life, The Legend,* as well as *What Would Audrey Do?* Her work has been featured on the *Today* show, *Larry King Live, Entertainment Tonight* and the BBC, and in *Vanity Fair, The New York Times, Town & Country, InStyle, People* magazine, *Harper's Bazaar,* the *Los Angeles Times* and hundreds of other media outlets around the world. A graduate of Vassar College, she lives in New York City. Her website is www.pamelakeogh.com.